D1079973

Heart Beat of Love

Patricia Brendel

ISBN 978-1-63844-867-9 (paperback)
ISBN 978-1-63844-868-6 (digital)

Copyright © 2021 by Patricia Brendel

All rights reserved. No part of this publication may be reproduced, distributed, or transmitted in any form or by any means, including photocopying, recording, or other electronic or mechanical methods without the prior written permission of the publisher. For permission requests, solicit the publisher via the address below.

Christian Faith Publishing, Inc.
832 Park Avenue
Meadville, PA 16335
www.christianfaithpublishing.com

Printed in the United States of America

Introduction

This is a true story. It reflects our daughter's experience with Pearson syndrome. You may ask yourself, "What is Pearson syndrome?" I prefer to give you a picture of a real-life walk with this syndrome versus giving you an in-depth and detailed look at research and medical terminology. I want to keep this as simple as I can, to help you better understand this very complicated love story.

Pearson syndrome is a very rare and generally fatal disease, affecting multiple organs and their functions. It is a condition that interrupts the bone marrow and pancreatic duties.

This syndrome may affect children in different fashions, and their experiences may be different, for not all are the same. As a matter of fact, this is so rare (as I was told) that only a handful worldwide have ever been diagnosed with this syndrome. So let us take a walk down my daughter's path with Pearson syndrome. You will become quite familiar and knowledgeable with her disease process as well as the *light* of life she walked. Faith and love remain!

Homecoming

October 1, 1996, was a day that we will keep as a treasure engraved in our hearts forever. My husband, Steve, and I brought a life into this forever revolving world. At that time, we never realized the special beauty and the special gift that we delivered would teach us about tremendous strength, about deep knowledge, about God's hope, about true faith, and about God's love—His unconditional love. We could not even begin to imagine, let alone understand, the depth of our gift. We named our little miracle child Elly Elizabeth. She weighed five pounds, eleven ounces, and she was eighteen inches in length. She was a gorgeous baby girl with dark black hair and big brown eyes. She was absolutely breathtaking! Her beauty reflected from her two sisters, Lindsey and Jesi. They were excited to have their little baby sister finally join our family. I remember the day we brought her home. I don't remember what the weather was that day, for I was so focused on Elly that I was oblivious to my surroundings. My husband was driving oh so carefully as Elly and I remained in the backseat buckled in for safety. Steve made sure that his baby girl had the safest ride home. As we arrived, her sisters were smiling, giggling, and of course filled with so much joy. They wanted to hold her right away. Her grandparents were also there to welcome her home. Steve and I stood proudly, watching our family happily absorbing its newest member.

In the Beginning... God

Let us talk a little about my pregnancy, which was unlike my previous pregnancies. I remember having morning sickness with my first daughter, Lindsey, which lasted my first trimester. I had evening sickness with my second daughter, Jesi, which also lasted throughout my first trimester. However, with Elly, I remained dizzy throughout my entire pregnancy. I had many sonograms that were perfectly normal. In the beginning of my first trimester, I remembered a very strong and constant pain that remained on the right lower section of my abdomen. I was lying on the couch in tremendous fear, praying to God that I would not lose our baby. I felt a sense of doom. This pain seemed to last forever; however, I believe the pain lasted for twenty minutes or so. I never felt that pain again. During my last trimester, I was anemic, and I was prescribed iron. When I was informed of Elly's illness, I was told that I should have miscarried.

However, she decided to take another route in which she chose life. I realized that we were blessed with this special child for a reason. You will understand this statement as we continue on this pathway. I remember always thanking God for my blessings of having healthy children. I prayed every evening, asking God for health, safety, and protection of my children and husband. My prayer still remains, howbeit I pray differently now. *Now* I pray without fear and worry, for I have no reservations that my God is near, and I do not have to carry my baggage alone. In fact, I don't have to carry it at all. I just need to give it to the Lord.

Elly

Elly was born the smallest of our children. The *old wives' tale* states that each child born will be bigger in size. This was not true in our case. Our first daughter weighed six pounds, fourteen ounces and was nineteen and a half inches in length. Our second daughter weighed seven pounds, two ounces and was twenty inches in length. As you have read, Elly was our smallest.

After Elly's delivery, she experienced hypothermia. Her body temperature was under the normal range. She was treated with the heat lamp for a twelve-hour period, and blankets were applied. Elly and I were discharged twenty-four hours after delivery. Her examination upon discharge was graded healthy. Her first checkup with her pediatrician was a little alarming, for her weight decreased to five pounds, three ounces. I was instructed to keep her daily weight recorded by using our local grocery store scale until I could buy or borrow a pediatric scale. Naturally, between Elly's pediatrician and myself, we kept a very close eye on her weight. I weighed Elly as instructed. It was amusing putting my daughter onto the grocery store scale. I was fully aware of the reactions of the people around me—some inquisitive, some judgmental, and some in shocked amazement. I would giggle inside and shrug it off, for I knew it was for the good of my daughter. Since I know that people love to gossip, I just figured I had given them a unique story to take home to their families.

Three days after visiting her pediatrician, Elly became jaundiced, but I was told that everything was okay. I kept in very close contact with her pediatrician. He was an absolute angel in disguise. God puts in our pathway people to help and guide us. Elly was considered to be a winter baby, for she always had nasal congestion. Of course, we followed the doctor's orders to run a humidifier. She received her first set of baby shots when she was two months of age.

I breastfed Elly for the first six weeks of her life, but her weight was not increasing as we would have hoped. I also had suspicions of a condition called gastric reflux. This is a condition where the acid in the stomach causes pain and inflammation in the esophagus. The symptoms she was having consisted of crying after eating with projectile vomiting or spitting up, choking, and arching of the back after she ate. Elly always threw her head back and screamed in pain. I would panic during these episodes. A mother has a special bond with her child, and I knew something was very, *very* wrong. I spoke with her pediatrician, and he suggested we start her on baby formula in hopes of weight gain and to help lessen her reflux by thickening her formula. She also slept in an upright angle in her crib. We elevated her mattress, and her pediatrician suggested that we start her out on a predigested formula, Alimentum, and thicken it with rice cereal. Elly's weight at two weeks was up to five pounds, eleven ounces, and she was nineteen inches in length. She was gaining weight!

Two Months of Age

Her story begins: Elly's symptoms began to appear on December 13. I remember taking Elly to visit her pediatrician, for she was showing signs of a cold and a low-grade fever. That time, we visited with the nurse practitioner. I remember speaking to the nurse with such great detail. I always had my children's symptoms written down prior to their pediatrician visits. This day was no exception. I explained that my daughter's breathing was quite rapid, and the color of her skin was pasty pale. My instinct was correct. During our visit to the pediatrician's office, Elly and I made a few trips back and forth between the doctor's office, lab, and the emergency room. Thank goodness they were all within walking distance. First, we were sent to the lab to check for a respiratory infection. We waited at the pediatrician's office for the results. As we were waiting, the nurse practitioner noticed that her color was becoming even more pale and pasty. Elly's temperature was taken indicating a higher fever. The nurse wanted to converse with one of the other doctors for his opinion. Elly and I went back over to the lab for a complete blood workup. It was explained when an infant under three months of age has a fever and is demonstrating signs of illness that this is unusual and that they would like to check her blood. Infants up to three months of age usually do not become sick, for they still have the mother's antibodies to help fight infection. We were instructed to wait in the emergency room for the results of the lab work.

As I recall, we were waiting for quite a while. I attempted to feed her, but she was rejecting the bottle. We were still awaiting the results, which seemed like an eternity before we would hear any news. As Elly and I were waiting in one of the cubicles at the ER,

I overheard a nurse talking in a loud voice. I can't remember word for word what she said, but it was something in the order of "Oh my God, that poor little girl." I remember saying to Elly as I walked and rocked with her, "Oh we should pray for this little one, for she must be very ill." I never expected it to be my daughter! The nurse came back into the room and explained that Elly had a severe case of anemia. Elly's hemoglobin was 5.3. The normal range is 9.4 to 13.0. Her hematocrit was 17.7. The normal range is 28 to 42. Elly and I went back over to the doctor's office and once again waited to hear from one of the doctors.

I can't express how wonderful the pediatrician's staff treated Elly and me. I am forever grateful for the kindness and love they demonstrated. They showed much compassion and understanding and gave excellent medical care. They were simply very kind. The combined horror and fear that I felt inside was not only inexpressible but equally unexplainable. The doctor explained to me that the reason it took so long for the results is that they were testing for leukemia. Thank God it was negative. I was in shock! I asked again, "What did you check for?" At that time, I began to weep, for I realized that my baby was the sick little girl who needed all of my love and prayers. I asked the doctor, "Will she be all right?" His response was "I don't know." I appreciated his honesty.

At this time, Elly was admitted to the hospital for a blood transfusion. Imagine your child needing a blood transfusion at such an early age when she was supposed to be healthy! It was truly terrifying. I remember thinking at one point that I was taking my daughter to see the doctor for something I believed was minor. Now my family and I are faced with a fear of the unknown. I was instructed to sign release forms to allow them to administer the blood. I was so frightened of the blood, wondering if it might be tainted with HIV, AIDS, hepatitis, etc. A mother protects her child with every fiber of her existence. This was a very difficult decision. It was explained that if this blood transfusion was not administered now that my family and I could lose our baby. This brought a completely different light into perspective. I signed without hesitation, and I prayed to God to help my daughter and keep her safe. I knew from here on, my daughter was in God's hands. Three days later, Elly's hemoglobin was 11.6, and her hematocrit was 35.2. We were thrilled! The hemoglobin and the hematocrit deal with the blood levels and the oxygen levels that are within the blood.

Elly's Love Journey Begins

We were in this fight together, and together we would remain. Our family remained inseparable. Elly found comfort in our arms, and we found comfort holding her. Remember with every heart beat is *love*!

December of *1996*, Elly was hospitalized for ten days due to a gastrointestinal virus. Her first Christmas was spent in the hospital. Through this hospital stay, her hemoglobin remained within normal limits, but her acid levels were high. Her acid level was treated by a base in the attempt to stabilize it. She was dehydrated due to vomiting and continuous diarrhea. Was this enough to throw her acid levels off? Let us continue reading. The hospital stays were an adjustment not only for Elly but for our family as well. Elly was able to spend her first New Year's Eve at home, and we were very excited to have our family together for this holiday!

Three Months of Age

January 13, 1997, Elly was tested for gastric reflux, for her symptoms were becoming worse. This testing lasted eighteen hours. I stayed with her, playing, reading books, and rocking to comfort her. Reflux was diagnosed on January 15. At this time, two medications were given. She was prescribed Zantac, Propulsid, and thickened formula. Gastric reflux is the result of acid in your stomach rising up through the esophagus, causing burning, spitting up, projectile vomiting, and pain. Elly would literally arch her back and scream in pain. After the reflux testing was completed, a more detailed blood test (CBC or complete blood count) was ordered (see Resource and Definition page). She was now referred by her pediatrician to see a pediatric hematologist at Children's Hospital because her hemoglobin was decreasing.

January 18, a bone marrow study was performed at Children's Hospital. Elly weighed nine pounds, seven ounces. Her bone marrow study revealed irregular-shaped blood cells. These cells were not functioning correctly. On January 20, Elly had another blood transfusion. This time when her blood was taken, it was sent to a New York laboratory for testing. One week after the transfusion, her hemoglobin was holding steady. We were so happy!

Her retic count was 1.1. This is the count that shows how many red blood cells are being produced. (The normal range for the retic count is 0.9 to 2.1.) The hematologist wanted to keep a close eye on her blood count; therefore, she had multiple tests. By the time February 3 rolled around, her hemoglobin was 9.1. It was coming down. Her retic count was also coming down with a count of 0.4. At this point, Elly is now four months of age. At her next blood check, her hemoglobin had decreased to 8.0. It had been about a week since her previous check.

Four Months of Age

February 10 was a day of uncertainty. This was the day Elly was diagnosed with Pearson syndrome. When the doctor began to explain the process of this syndrome, all my husband and I heard was there is *no cure*. The hematologist kept talking and stating that this is a fatal disease. Unfortunately, the news was not what we were expecting, nor was the outcome. At that point, neither my husband nor myself heard all the medical information. We just could not comprehend what he was trying to tell us. It was like we were in the room with the doctor watching his lips move but couldn't hear a word he was saying. All we heard was *no cure* and she was going to *die*. Those words echoed through our minds, shutting out all other attempts of communication. Devastation filled us, and we wept. After the shock subsided, we made up our minds that we would fight! Our daughter was strong and was a fighter. We learned from her how to move forward with strength and love. That is exactly what we did through prayer, faith, hope, and love.

I aggressively sought out the doctor whom I considered to be an expert on this syndrome in order to help my daughter. It took many attempts, but then one day, I finally was able to connect with him. I remember asking him many questions, and all he could say is "I am sorry." He stated that the only medical advice he could give was to manage the symptoms and assured me that the team was doing all they could. I was hoping for more information; however, I did not give up on hope. As I have learned, Pearson syndrome deals with many parts of the body. This is why we use the word "syndrome" over "disease," for it is not one particular body part that is being attacked. This dreadful syndrome attacked multiple body functions. Each child's symptoms vary with this syndrome. Per statistic, there were only a handful of children in the US that had ever been diagnosed with this syndrome and an estimate of sixty cases in the world. As for Elly, it was attacking her bone marrow, not allowing her body to fight against infection or bad cells. The bone marrow deals with blood functions. This syndrome was attacking her pancreas, not allowing her to digest food properly, which in the future would affect her insulin.

As we delved deeper, we realized that this syndrome created a serious cell deficiency, which manifests itself in the bone marrow and pancreas (see *mitochondria* on Resource and Definition page). With any mitochondrial disease, disturbances arise like acidosis (this has to do with the acid levels in your body) and the loss of electrolytes. This entailed in Elly's condition the loss of major sodium levels, which caused acidosis. Understand that once your electrolytes are imbalanced, your system starts to compensate for what you may be lacking. In Elly's case, her breathing would become rapid and labored. This would cause her total carbon dioxide levels to drop. Normal range for carbon dioxide level is 21 to 32. Hers would drop between 13 to 17. When her carbon dioxide would hit 18, we would be happy.

Pearson syndrome also has a high risk for sepsis and then death. This syndrome is very involved and dangerous. We were ready and willing to fight with our very being.

We dealt with the genetics department, neurology department, and the endocrinology department, as well as the hematologist and pediatrician. In the future, we will add another specialist—a gastroenterologist. Elly was put on numerous medications such as Carnitor, Coenzyme Q-10, and a pancreatic enzyme. This does not include her acid reflux medications. The Carnitor and Coenzyme Q-10 were to help with the metabolic issues and the pancreatic enzymes were to aid in digestion.

So as you can see, Elly had a team of doctors that were in charge of her care. I came to know the team very well. Hence, I became the care coordinator. Steve and I were adamant and aggressive concerning Elly's medical care. After all, this was our child. Having as many doctors as Elly did, information had to be given to all, to keep them on the same page. During her care, it was mentioned that we enroll her in a research clinic for lactic acidosis. Elly's lactic acid was very high, which was cause for alarm. Normal lactic acid is 0.8 to 1.8. Hers would run around 11 and 12, making her a candidate for this type of research. The drug or medication which would have been given was an experimental drug. There had not been much research behind this drug at this point. My husband and I thought long and hard on this research program. The one agreement that we shared was not to put Elly through any more than what was needed, nor did we want her to be an experimental specimen. She would have undergone a series of tests, which would involve blood, spinal fluid taps, fasting, etc. Elly was not able to fast, for this would have caused an imbalance in her electrolytes, causing acidosis, sugar drops, and more. Weighing the risks, we turned it down. In the back of our minds, we wondered if we were making the right decision. As you can see, in Elly's care, there weren't any right or wrong decisions. It was called mother's intuition, parent intuition if you will. As I said before, we remained in faith, hope, and love.

Pneumonia settled in on February 13. Elly's hemoglobin dropped to 8. She was pale. Breathing treatments were being administered at home. Her appetite was poor. Running through my mind was the nutrition aspect, which was one major concern of this syndrome. Her mental progress was developing well. She was age appropriate. Her weight and growth were poor. She weighed eight pounds, fourteen ounces and was twenty-two inches in length. At four months of age, Elly was smiling, cooing, reaching, clasping fingers, rolling from side to side, and taking a pacifier in and out of her beautiful mouth.

Our family made a trip to Children's Hospital for additional tests and another blood transfusion. Elly had numerous blood transfusions. As I stated earlier, our family would fight this syndrome together. Her father and uncle were so gracious to donate their blood, for their blood type matched Elly's blood type. Steve and his brother alternated donating blood as she would need many transfusions. I am so very grateful for their humility and the very special gift that they gave—blood. During this hospital stay, her blood sugar test was normal. Her spinal tap showed that the lactic acid in her body was 9.6 higher than what was in her brain, which was 6. Remember the normal range is 0.8 to 1.8. This was a good sign for the lactic acid in her brain was lower, giving her a better chance for brain development. Elly tolerated her hospital visits very well, and she smiled even though she was exhausted.

On February 25, Elly was hospitalized due to wheezing. She was hooked up to an apnea monitor and continued with breathing treatments. During this hospital stay, we experienced a terrifying episode where Elly's eyes became blank, and she did not move. I had no idea what was happening, but in an instant, I called for help, and the nurses came rushing in! The doctor felt that this episode was due to her reflux. She continued to receive breathing treatments at home, along with her other prescribed medications. This treatment continued for the rest of her life. With this syndrome, she would produce phlegm. This phlegm would sometimes become very thick where a Toothette was needed to remove it from her throat. She did have a few times where she would stop breathing until this phlegm was removed. A bulb syringe was also used to clear her nose of drainage. These procedures had to be done carefully not to cause irritation of the nose or irritation of blood vessels that would begin bleeding.

I kept record of Elly's food intake and output such as vomiting, bowel movements, urine output, crying, etc. This was completed on a daily basis to report to the doctors if any adjustments needed to be made on her food and formula. If she would have any of the above, this would put her at risk for lactic acidosis. We tried to keep her as happy as possible. This was not really a hard task.

As mentioned prior, weight gain is very important for Elly's health. At five months of age, she weighed eight pounds. We are not only looking at pounds but ounces as well, for ounces are very important to her health. I recorded her weight on a daily basis to report to her doctors.

Make A Wish Foundation contacted our family, for they wanted to give Elly a wish. This is an extremely wonderful foundation for children with terminal illnesses. These people have a caring, nurturing heart who put forth their love and support. They truly make children's wishes come true. I give them many thanks for their support with our daughter. Their gift to Elly was a comfort wish. Elly loved to rock, so we received a rocker glider chair with an ottoman. We spent hours in this chair. I have to say this was her favorite spot as well as mine, sitting there rocking together. They also provided us with a stroller, which hooked on to the back of a bike. This stroller had a shield, which protected her from the wind, bugs, etc. She loved going for walks. Our whole family enjoyed our time outside together.

At this point, Elly had not been producing any sounds, but on March 13, she laughed for the very first time! We were so excited! Even as Elly would progress, she would quickly digress with her illnesses or hospital stays, which is normal. We call these setbacks. What we needed to keep in mind is that her deformities were on the inside of her body. Her body on the outside was beautiful!

Children with any type of mitochondrial disease are soothed by warmth. The warmth helps to ease their pain. Now, what I need to explain for you so you better understand this statement is that lactic acid is produced by exercising, very hard workouts, crying, etc. This is what makes your muscles sore, painful, and hurt. After a long hard aerobic workout, you wonder why you may hurt or your muscles are in pain. This is due to your lactic acid. Elly had these symptoms on a continuous basis, for her levels were always high. Cuddling and warmth helped and soothed her. Everyone in our family thoroughly enjoyed taking their turns cuddling her, including myself, my husband, her sisters, and her grandparents.

Five Months of Age

On March 14, Elly was admitted to Children's Hospital during a routine visit. Her white blood count and neutrophil count were extremely low, which means she was not able to fight against any type of infection. The normal range of a white blood count is between 5.0 to 20. Elly's count was 1. The normal range of neutrophil is between 2.0 to 7.5. Elly's was 0 (zero). This was extremely alarming for the team of doctors as she was running a low-grade temperature as well. This hospitalization lasted four days. Elly also had another blood transfusion during this stay. Her weight was now up to nine pounds, eight ounces.

When we woke up on March 20, I noticed Elly's breathing was very rapid and hard. She was making a grunting noise. I knew within the very depth of my soul that *our baby was in trouble*! I called the pediatrician to announce we were on our way. By the time we arrived, her breathing had become worse. I ran to the nurse and explained what was happening, and oxygen was applied. The doctor examined her, and off to the hospital we went for admission. I was fighting my feelings, for I knew my baby was fighting for her life! Helplessness enveloped me. The control was out of my hands and out of my husband's hands. I ran to God! Prayer is very powerful! A sense of helplessness always had a way of returning; however, I stood on my faith and hope. This faith is what gave me the courage and strength I needed for our daughter. At this point, Elly was listed as critical. Today we almost lost her, but with the love of God, she lived. She was extremely acidotic; she had no blood sugar and was very dehydrated. Her blood gases (carbon dioxide) were extremely low. They worked with our daughter all day. As I watched them work with her, all I could see was how limp and lifeless she was. I tried so very hard to stay strong, but the emotion of possibly losing a child came crashing down on me so fast I was not able to think. All I could do was pray and cry. At this point, I felt numb. I thank my mom for being there by my side comforting me. The doctors and nurses were absolutely medical warriors, for they were able to stabilizer her. She was hospitalized for seven days. I never left her side nor did her daddy. We would take turns staying with her in the hospital while trying to keep a somewhat normal life for our other daughters.

Our daughters never knew if Elly and I would be home when they arrived home from school. My heart was broken as a mother. It is hard to be divided and separated. I knew they were in amazing hands, for my husband and parents provided the love and support they needed when I was not able to be there.

We never left Elly's side, for our belief was that if she felt our love and our strength that she would continue to fight. We did this continually. Elly was being given IV fluids, but her doctors wanted to experiment to see how her body would react without them. After one day without IV fluids, she became dehydrated. The fluids were resumed immediately. The next step was to try to wean her off the fluids slowly, but the same results were happening—dehydration.

Our priest came to see us on Good Friday. He blessed her. He sat and talked with us for quite some time, prayerfully sharing his love, compassion, and understanding. He definitely was a man of God. Now understand, this was Easter weekend, and he had masses to prepare for, but he unselfishly spent all day with us. Elly was discharged on Holy Saturday. I was uneasy, for she continued to vomit and have diarrhea, and her appetite was poor, but we still asked the doctor if we could try going home for Easter. Holy Saturday was a little rocky, but by the time Easter Sunday arrived, Elly was unbelievably better! We all had a wonderful day. She ate that day and kept all of her food down. She napped and was getting her rest. She did not have any bowel movements. Our family had a very blessed day together, for this was her very first Easter. This was a miracle Easter!

During this horrifying experience between life and death, my husband and I were approached with a "No Code" documentation. The medical staff thought it may be in our best interest as well as our daughter's if there came a time when they felt no more could be done. As her parents, the love bond between our hearts and souls were so strong, the answer was *no*. I explained to them that I expected nothing less than for them to do everything in their power to keep our daughter alive. Please understand, I respect the medical field very much; however, they looked only into the scientific methods of her diagnosis. They were not able to look past the scientific into the supernatural. I kept reminding all the doctors on her team that we, as a family, would stand on love, faith, and hope. We believe in miracles. We believe in our God, and we truly lived a miracle with our daughter. I will make this statement now. God saved our daughter. His hand was not the one who had caused this illness, but it was His hand that had saved her.

Six Months of Age

The team started Elly on Neupogen injections. These injections would help increase her white blood count. They were prescribed for two to three times a week, depending on her count. Epogen injections were also introduced. These injections were to help increase her red blood cells. These were discontinued over time, for they did not help as had been expected. Elly's pediatric nurse came to give these injections. She had numerous duties in helping our daughter. When you picture this story, picture our home as an intensive care unit. Her doctors wanted me to learn to give her the injections. However, as her mother, I was not willing to give her any medical care, unless in an emergency. I was my daughter's security, and I wanted to remain focused in that role. Elly had gained weight again. Hallelujah! She now weighed in at nine pounds, eleven ounces while remaining at twenty-three inches in length. We were thrilled for the increase!

As our journey continued, Elly experienced fluctuations in her weight and blood work. Medications, blood transfusions, and life were adjusted accordingly. With every step, we remained hopeful in our Lord, and prayer became an essential part of our family.

Since Elly was in need of many blood transfusions, her daddy and uncle had become her donors at alternating times, as mentioned earlier. They matched Elly's blood type of A+. Our family is truly blessed for the love that we share. We had so much support and prayers. I believe prayer is powerful. When I look back on the road we've traveled, I realized many miracles have occurred. As far as any type of reactions to the blood transfusions, she only had one, which was minor, and we were able to continue with these.

It was Elly and I that made numerous trips to her doctor appointments. She had many, so the doctors thought it best that we had an apnea monitor for traveling and sleeping purposes. As mentioned earlier, Elly would stop breathing because of the immensely thick phlegm that she produced due to her illness. To meet safety regulations, Elly's car seat had to be secured into the backseat, facing backward. The monitor would also decrease my stress level since I was not able to see my daughter's face. We also invested in a mirror, which helped at times, but the fact was I needed to keep my eyes on the road. So this apnea monitor was a lifesaver.

Elly was growing. She was now up to eleven pounds and was now twenty-four inches in length. Within a few weeks, her weight dropped to ten pounds, fourteen ounces, and her hemoglobin had decreased to 7.6. She would need another blood transfusion soon, for her symptoms of paleness, rapid breathing, tremors, and weakness were beginning to appear. It was time now for the transfusion.

Seven Months of Age

On May 1, Elly's sisters took her for a walk in their baby doll stroller. Elly herself was not much bigger than a baby doll. The girls had so much fun this day playing together. Elly absolutely loved it! As a matter of fact, she was determined to stay in the baby doll stroller, so she took a nap there. Elly's sisters were at her beck and call. They loved her very much, and whatever their sister needed, they did for her. Elly loved music. She and her sisters would listen to music and dance. I came across a beautiful plaque that read "Music is well said to be the speech of angels." How true! This I must say was Elly's favorite pastime. When Elly was happy, she would give such a bright beautiful smile with a little snoot that she made with her nose. Elly didn't laugh out loud, but she certainly presented us with an adorable snooty smile, and then we knew she was enjoying every minute of our play, reading books, dancing to music, or whatever activity we were doing at that time. Elly never communicated with words, but as a family, we communicated through sign language and nonverbal methods.

On May 16, Elly was exposed to chicken pox! I felt the fear envelop me. The doctors were very concerned, for they were not sure how her immune system would defend her against this childhood disease. A series of gamma globulin injections were started, not only with Elly but with her sisters and daddy too. Her father was not sure if he ever had chicken pox, so to play it safe, he received this series. These shots would help reduce their risk and reduce the risk of death for Elly. My one daughter who came down with chicken pox was miserable. As a family, we managed just fine and conquered this disease. During this process, the doctors wanted to see if her reflux had been relieved. We found out she still needed to be on Propulsid. We were hoping to decrease some of her medication intake. A few weeks later, our other daughter came down with chicken pox. Elly once again needed the gamma globulin shots. I laughed, for the series of shots my daughter and husband received did not eliminate the risk for them, but this daughter's outbreak was not so severe. As for my husband and Elly, no sign of chicken pox.

Eight Months of Age

On June 1, *Elly* was having an amazing day. No complaints, and her appetite was back. I was so happy! However, two days later, Elly came down with chicken pox! Panic had risen, and I called the pediatrician immediately. He was an amazing doctor, and I called him her "hero" doctor. She was started on the gamma globulin shot along with her Neupogen shots. Also, she was given Tylenol for pain. The Neupogen injection was given for five days along with a viral medication. Elly had a total of fifty pox. She had an appointment every day until this process was complete. As I look back, I realized that as a parent and a mother, you become so involved in your child's care that you don't have time to fear, *but* you have time to rise up and keep on loving her and moving forward. You move forward with all your heart and soul.

I remember praying to God to take this syndrome from her and added that if someone needed to bear this, I would. I begged and pleaded. I would have done anything and everything for her. Unfortunately, I was not able to take her pain and suffering away. I settled for the next best thing and loved her with all my might and my heart. We cuddled, we rocked, I sang to her, and I gave her my all, but most importantly, I gave her *love* and compassion. I refused to accept death! I prayed and kept the hope. I kept the heart beat of love. By June 7, the chicken pox had ended. She made it through by the grace of God. By the way, at this age, she began her teething process! Do you know how her symptoms were handled? With love.

Nine Months of Age

July 1, Elly blossomed. Her weight was twelve pounds, eight ounces, and her blood work was normal. Understand, Elly had normal childhood sicknesses as well. I recall ear infections and pink eye. At those times, antibiotics were added to her other medications. At this age, she was diagnosed with photophobia, which only means she is sensitive to light. Her ophthalmologist prescribed sunglasses with dark lenses. They worked for her; however, she did not like wearing them. So as you can see, an ophthalmologist was added to the team of doctors.

Elly begins to speak! On July 12, she said "dada," and the next day, she said "baba." Our entire family clapped, for she brought so much joy into our lives. The doctors were always amazed by her. They never knew what to think or expect, for they never knew what her God-given capabilities were. She proved them wrong time and time again in their thinking and expectations.

On July 14, Elly received her six-month baby shots plus her Neupogen shot. Keep in mind, she was behind on her immunizations due to her syndrome. As time went on, the team met and agreed that there would be no more immunizations for Elly unless they were dead vaccines. Moving forward, Elly's communication is improving little by little, word by word. She said "up." Once again, we were overjoyed.

Our family took our first trip together to an amusement park. Elly and her sisters enjoyed the merry-go-round. She enjoyed riding the kiddie rides. That day, we noticed that her eyes were becoming more sensitive to light, but she would not wear her sunglasses. She was, however, still having a wonderful day. Her appetite was good, her bowels normal, and she was now napping. The next day, we went to see her hematologist and her pediatric eye doctor. This doctor felt that she had glaucoma and needed to measure her eye. Elly wasn't very cooperative. Imagine a little one sitting still to have her eye pressure measured. She was not having it, and to be truthful, neither was her father. So the eye doctor mentioned the only way to have an accurate reading would be to put her under anesthetic. That meant that Elly was not able to drink or eat anything until this procedure was completed. This is a problem. Children of any type of mitochondrial disease should not be put under any type of anesthesia due to underlying conditions. The anesthesia may bring out other problems relating to mitochondria, which sometimes do lay dormant and will bring these problems to life. It also brings out the mitochondrial myopathy, which means they will stop breathing. Once again, we are faced with a decision. If we didn't do this procedure, Elly could go blind. If we do this procedure, other problems could arise. It seemed to my husband and myself that not only were we disturbed about all of this, but the anesthesiologist was also. As a matter of fact, the anesthesiologist said, "I will not put her under due to her syndrome."

The one main concern that we were always faced with was this: Elly had many doctors, and these specialists were absolutely amazing in their individual areas of expertise.

However, when it came to a team session, they seemed to be unwilling to compromise their individual beliefs in order to collaborate effectively with the other specialists. The fact remains that there is not enough research on this syndrome for the doctors to relate to. Therefore, it was difficult keeping the team on the same page with all her diagnoses, medication changes, hospitalizations, etc. I believe that most of these doctors just didn't know what to do or where to turn. There was always one dilemma or another. As her mother, I kept them all on board on the process of her syndrome, whether it was by day or by hour or by minute.

Now back to the glaucoma testing. Elly had gone a few hours without eating. The eye doctor had been running into one snag after another, causing more delays. One snag was finding an anesthesiologist. Now keep in mind when Elly didn't drink her bottle with medicine and eat her food, she came under the threat of becoming acidotic. So much time had passed, and it was now approximately 7:00 p.m. when the eye doctor suggested we come back the next morning at 6:30 a.m. to do the procedure. We were three hours away, and as you can guess, we were extremely upset with the whole ordeal and drove home in complete exhaustion. Only one guess as to what happened next.

The following day, July 30, Elly had become very acidotic. Her breathing was impaired and very different from her usual breathing. Her breathing was hard and rapid. She was also dehydrated and was unable to keep any of her food or formula down. She was admitted to the hospital. Her sodium level was very low, and she was started on sodium bicarbonate immediately. Her electrolytes were off from the normal ranges, and her potassium was high. She had lost weight and was now down to twelve pounds, three ounces. She also received another blood transfusion. As stated before, we knew what would happen, but getting the physicians to hear and listen to us was another task. The admission was inevitable. As time went on, I learned and understood how to interact and get the physician's attention. You will understand this statement as you read on.

The team of physicians understood the full depth of the fasting process with a child who has Pearson syndrome. We were learning together. Medications were extremely important to keep her functioning and balanced. As time went on, it was explained to us why Elly loses a lot of sodium through her kidneys due to this syndrome. The way it was explained to us was this: each of her kidneys is like a bucket that has many, many holes in them not being able to contain the fluids, especially her sodium. This is called Fanconi syndrome, which is a part of Pearson syndrome. We just added another diagnosis to her list.

Ten Months of Age

On August 1, Elly stood by herself for the first time. This day was a beautiful day! Our family went outside for a walk, and we all enjoyed the outdoors. It had been a long time since we had been outside due to the photophobia which caused Elly discomfort. The next couple of days were joyous with no problems noted. We as a family enjoyed our time together.

On August 13, Elly fell for the very first time in her little life! She fell smack on her face causing her mouth to bleed and bleed and bleed. She lost a considerable amount of blood. I started to panic because I could not get the bleeding under control. Her father, who was calm, took her outside and walked around with her as he held pressure to her mouth. The bleeding stopped. Thank God for her daddy! It took close to twenty minutes before the bleeding stopped completely. As I explained this incident to her pediatrician, he stated that I needed to call him if and when this happens again due to her hemoglobin and low platelet count. The next day, Elly woke up with a very fat lip but in an excellent mood. As a matter of fact, Elly was babbling and laughing. Do you know what that does for a parent's heart to hear their child babbling and laughing when you normally don't hear that? It brings so much love and joy to their lives because of the preciousness of life, of love. I must say, when you look back on her life, she was an exceptional girl who definitely is a God-given gift. During this month, she said "*Mama*!" Was I excited? Oh my goodness…*I was ecstatic*! This mother beamed all day, and I was so aware of my love for my husband and my daughters. Love surrounds us each and every day. All we need to do is recognize this. This love goes farther than any other measure. It went on in our lives back then, and it remains in our lives now. However, in a stronger measure. In God's measure.

Elly had a specialized instructional teacher that came into our home through the state program of Early Intervention Services. She was an amazing and compassionate woman. Elly so enjoyed playing with her, for she didn't realize the work they were accomplishing. She also had a speech therapist whom she also enjoyed, although not necessarily her teaching "techniques." She had a texture issue, and she didn't like anything foreign in her mouth. As time went on, other techniques were used to help with texture issues.

The Early Intervention Services is an amazing program, and they help many little ones. As for Elly, she enjoyed her time with them; however, there were many interruptions due to her hospitalizations. They were very patient and compassionate. Elly would make leaps and bounds in development and then digress when hospitalized. This is a normal process. However, the therapists never gave up on her, and for that, I thank them wholeheartedly with love.

Elly was now becoming more aware of her surroundings, and she was beginning to miss her sisters when they left for school. She certainly seemed to know the time of their arrival from school. She would wait for them, and upon seeing them, she would become very excited and clap her hands. Well of course, we know what would happen next. They would run into the house, bypassing their mommy, running to their sister with all the love in the world, and they would play, laugh, cuddle, and love on one another with joy.

Eleven Months of Age

On September 1, Elly started out having a terrible appetite, and she was very gassy. The next day, she began with a cough. She seemed as though she was not getting better, so I made an appointment with her pediatrician's office, and off we went. Please keep in mind, we live in a rural country area, and her pediatrician was an hour away.

Her specialists were three hours away. We arrived at her appointment. Her weight was now twelve pounds, fourteen ounces. She received a Rocephin shot to help prevent any type of infection that may be brewing. The next day, she seemed to be doing better. She had a wonderful morning, and her disposition was wonderful. Her appetite was better, but her bowel movements were phlegmy. Elly's mornings remained consistent for a week now.

She was still throwing up, and she was very congested. She now was breathing through her mouth. It seemed as though she was making more and more phlegm. On September 6, she received another Rocephin shot and a decongestant. The next day, Elly continued to have phlegmy vomit, and her bowel movements were loose. This was a red flag. But we stayed in love and kept on loving her. Within two days, the symptoms seemed to turn around, and she was happy. She started eating baby food again. How wonderful it was to see her eat! For this developmental process was a struggle. We were overjoyed! Two weeks later, Elly had become pale; however, this was coming and going. Once again, this is a flag that we needed to monitor closely, for her paleness could lead into breathing issues very quickly.

On September 14, Elly was playing on her own, and she was having a good time. She also had three bites of a cookie, meaning she had actually chewed it up and swallowed it! We were thrilled! This is the first time she ever chewed and swallowed food! She had an amazing evening. By September 15, she was up to thirteen pounds, two ounces. She still had a good appetite. Hallelujah! The next few days were good. On September 20, she began to get fussy. We thought this may be due to the teething process. Of course, we weren't sure. She had also begun increased vomiting, she stopped eating, and she became miserable. With this, her breathing became rapid, so I put sodium bicarbonate in her bottle. This was prescribed for instances such as this. What does sodium bicarbonate mean? It helped keep her electrolytes in check, especially her sodium levels, which go awry when vomiting is in excess. The next day, she woke up, and her two front teeth were swollen. We were correct in thinking it was the teething process, but we couldn't let our guard down with her symptoms for they could change in a heart beat. We were always on intuition alert! Now, please don't misunderstand me, we took the good with the bad, and we kept moving forward. Elly's appetite was fair, but she was still not feeling well, and she was very gaggy. That means that now she was not eating as we would like her to.

September 22. Elly was weighed today. Her weight had dropped to twelve pounds, six ounces. I became very concerned. As I have mentioned before, when Elly was in trouble, I knew it. The next day, her morning had become worse than the day before. She was very irritable and cranky. She cried. We never wanted this to happen, for it would raise her lactic acid, causing lactic acidosis. She was acting very hungry, but she couldn't eat.

Thank goodness her blood gases were normal. However, her breathing was rapid, and she had a low-grade fever. She continued with her vomiting, which had increased. My daughter was in trouble.

Terror 2 Begins

When morning arrived, Elly was demonstrating signs of tachycardia, which is a very fast heart rate. She was very pale and breathing exceptionally fast and gasping for air. I frantically called my mother at work and said, "Elly is in trouble. I will pick you up! *Mom, she is in trouble*!"

I am very thankful that my mom was able to assist in times like these. My parents were definitely godsent. I am very thankful for mom's supervisor also for being so supportive and for giving her permission to leave during these emergencies. By the time I picked up my mom, who was thirty minutes away, Elly's condition had not changed. However, by the time we drove the additional thirty minutes to the pediatrician's office, her breathing had become much worse. She was admitted to the hospital for dehydration. At this time, no one seemed to be very worried. As for me, I was extremely uneasy and knew deep down in my heart that this was extremely serious. As I have said time and time again, mothers know their children and they should always follow their heart. My mom, Elly, and I were in the hospital room when I said, "Mom, there is something seriously wrong here, for I can *feel* it." At that moment, Elly shrieked in pain, and her eyes went completely blank (black), then she had no response. I yelled for the nurse, and she came running. I said, "Something needs to be done, something is wrong!" I felt as though she was having a seizure, but they were unable to determine this at that time. IVs were started ASAP, and the nurse suggested I call my husband.

Once again, my heart broke! I began to pray and pray, asking God for his help in healing our precious daughter. She was in serious condition. She was dehydrated and severely acidotic. Her electrolytes were out of control. About an hour had passed before Elly started to come back to us. Prior to that, she had laid on the bed with no reaction or response. I was so very happy to see our baby girl start to move, but I still felt uneasy. I knew she wasn't out of danger. A day or so later, her condition worsened. The nurses kept a very close eye on her, but I knew that wasn't going to be enough. All of the hospital staff, right down to the cleaning crew, were so very supportive and kind. We could not have asked for a more compassionate group of people. Elly started to cry again with such a shrieking sound which was the sound of pain. Her heart rate raised very quickly, and she was acting unusual. Her eyes looked vacant. I was terrified. I didn't know what to do or what to expect. What happens next is complete terror! After I settled her down that night, she gave a horrifying scream and threw up black acid. She went directly into a seizure. I screamed, and once again, the nurses came running into the room. I basically threw Elly into the arms of the first nurse that came through the door. I screamed, "*Please, please* help her, *please*!"

This experience is something I never, ever thought I would see. It is complete devastation when you are not able to help or comfort your child due to intense pain and symptoms that are out of your control. Thank goodness for *God*! I went directly to the Most High God. I prayed and continued to pray for a miracle that she would beat this disease and wake up completely well. I understand now that every day we had our Elly was a blessing and miracle from God. Her pediatrician was called, and he came as fast as he could drive. He evaluated her and the situation. I was told to call the rest of my family to come to the hospital right away, but I knew I wasn't able. A nurse called my aunt who lived nearby and asked her to come immediately. I remember I was alone with Elly, and I melted. I don't know if a nurse or my aunt called my family, but I know they were advised to come *now*.

Remember they lived one hour away, and time was of the essence. Elly was listed in critical condition. We sat in the waiting room desperately waiting for the doctor's prognosis, and also the arrival of our family. Elly's pediatrician came into the lounge and explained to us that he was not sure, but he believed the bad mitochondrial cells had affected Elly's brain. He said I had two options: the first was to put her on a ventilator and life flight her to Children's Hospital and the second to keep her here and make her as comfortable as possible. Without hesitation, I told him to life flight her to Children's Hospital. Before the life flight crew arrived, Elly's daddy, sisters, grandparents, and uncle arrived. Elly started to come around, but she was in the danger zone. I asked to fly to the hospital with her, but I was unable to, for there was a six-person crew on board, and there was no room for me. I tried to understand, but just the same, they were taking my baby without me!

Before they prepped her, Elly's daddy and I went in and gave her a big kiss and hug, and we wished her a safe trip. We told her we would meet her at the hospital. The life flight crew was fantastic. They were very kind and started the process of prepping Elly for her trip. I watched them as they hooked her up to the ventilator and administered medicine for her seizures, along with a sedative for a noncomplicated ride. They explained every step to her father and me, for we did not leave her side until they were ready to leave. As any parent, I needed to know what exactly they were doing, even if I didn't understand the medical arena. They reassured us that she would be okay. Decisions had to be made, and emotions were very high. I knew that I had to pull myself together for our daughter in order to help her fight this syndrome, if you will, every step of the way.

So that is exactly what our family did! Elly's daddy, sisters, grandparents, and I drove three hours to Children's Hospital. My husband is an excellent driver. If I am not mistaken, we arrived twenty minutes after Elly. So this means Steve drove superfast. Of course, none of us minded, for we all arrived safely. We were not able to see her right away, for they were in the process of stabilizing her. They were very up front with us and explained to us that our daughter was a very sick little girl. We still remained hopeful! All of her doctors from Children's Hospital were notified.

It was a difficult situation, for we had a team of specialized doctors in all different areas of expertise, trying to keep them on the same page. It was a tough process, but we would have been willing to die for our child, so this little inconvenience wasn't anything to us. What my husband and I suggested was to have a meeting to discuss Elly's needs in detail and how we were going to keep everyone "in the know" of her condition at all times. The team decided to appoint Elly's mommy and daddy as the team leaders. This role was not going to be easy, and as one might say, considerably complicated and demanding, but it was doable.

Elly was severely dehydrated, severely acidotic, and malnourished. She could have died this very night, but I believe God answered our prayers. Amen. Thank You, Jesus!

She started to recover! It took a very long time. We stayed at Children's Hospital for approximately one month.

During this recovery period, decisions had to be made, which were very difficult. Unfortunately, these decisions had to be made "in the now" moment, for time was not on our side. I was not able to give thought to the decisions made. All I could do was react. As a matter of fact, my husband had not been able to be there during that time. However, he was now on his way to the hospital. My mom was with me at this time, and how very thankful I was to her.

So you may be asking, what were these decisions that had to be made? The doctors wanted to surgically insert not only a Broviac catheter but also a G-J tube. A G-J tube would enable food to bypass her stomach and go directly to the intestines for absorption. This would allow her to keep the food in her body to aid in nutrition, growth, and weight gain. Also, the G-J tube would help aid in the healing of the acid reflux, which would bypass her stomach, stopping the acid from going up into her esophagus. The offset of this procedure allows the threat of increased infections due to decreased WBC (white blood cell count). The whole picture was bleak, but if this had not been done, she would have died. The Broviac is the permanent solution for IV access. The multiple IVs were very hard to insert due to her having shallow and weak veins. This means when they inserted the needle into the vein, it could puncture or injure it, causing the blood to leak into the surrounding tissue. The Broviac catheter would eliminate this problem. Also, it would enable immediate access in an emergency.

Remember back when I discussed Elly's eye problem? Putting her under anesthesia could pose severe problems, such as to stop breathing without warning signs. Well, as you can see, we were faced with this anesthesia decision again. We didn't really have a choice when she was life flighted, but we had to make the choice now. I needed to weigh the pros and cons. I hesitated. I was frightened beyond belief, but I put my child's life into the hands of *God* and the surgeons. I remember asking one of the surgeons about the risks involved and if Elly would come out of surgery well. He said, "We will take good care of her." I felt somewhat better, but my inner being was trembling. At that point, my husband arrived, and we gave Elly a big kiss and hug and our love. We told her we would be waiting for her and we would see her soon. They took her into surgery. The surgery lasted approximately two and a half and three hours. Throughout this time, it seemed an eternity had passed. We prayed and waited. Elly made it through surgery! The surgeon said that she had done wonderfully. Elly's cheering section, which included my husband and myself, her sisters, grandparents, and uncle, could not wait to see her!

The G-J tube had been placed in her abdominal area, and the Broviac had been inserted into the right side of her chest. I could not wait until I could hold her, but I was not sure how to do that without dislodging the tubes or causing discomfort. I know this probably sounds absurd, but seeing these foreign objects in my child, I just couldn't bear the thought of hurting her in any way. So with extreme tenderness, I picked her up to give her a big kiss and hug. I gently cuddled her until it was time for her to lie down. Her recovery went very well.

Up until this time, I was able to journal daily events. However, as the new path of this journey began, I found myself in what seemed like a whirlwind. Please understand that Elly had been in the ICU two times this visit. When we were on the pediatric floor, she would experience good days and bad days. As I mentioned before, the doctors, nurses, etc. were apprehensive of her syndrome. They had no idea what they were up against or what would happen next. Did any of this make sense to them? No. Remember, the doctors told us that in all reality, I should have miscarried in my first trimester due to her cells not developing correctly. However, Elly had a strong will to live and made miscarriage not an option. Her cells took a different route out of the ordinary. You see, instead of her cells taking the normal path, they took a path all of their own to give her life. Normally when there is a discrepancy in the cell formation, you miscarry. Now the question was, how long would this path that her cells had taken be able to last? This goes into so much more detail, that it would only become confusing if I try to explain any more than I already have. This stands to reason though. Even the doctors can't explain it all. I believe I would not be able to understand the depth of this syndrome either, but when it came to my daughter, I understood with my heart.

As we were admitted to the pediatric floor, I overheard a few nurses on that shift ask to be removed from her case for they were fearful of her condition. Elly's condition took up a tremendous amount of time, not only having medications administered on the hour, every hour, but making sure her Broviac and G-J tube sites were clean and functioning properly. They needed to keep a close eye on her weight gain or loss. How did they do this? By monitoring food intake, IV fluid intake, as well as urine and stool output.

Blood gases along with CBC (complete blood count) needed to be taken frequently to keep up to date on her blood levels and electrolytes, for as we know her condition could change in a heart beat. So basically, Elly needed a one-on-one nurse. This was impossible for the hospital nurses, for they had other patients to care for, and there was a nursing shortage. I understood the position the nurses were in, so I was educated on how to work the IV pump along with the feeding pump, which would prove to be essential in her care at home. I learned to titrate (increase and decrease) her amount of fluids and how to hook up and run the systems. I was extremely nervous, especially when it came to her IV pump, which connected to the Broviac line, and this line goes directly to her heart. I was very grateful for the education and training I received in the hospital. We took one day at a time. As a matter of fact, we took one hour at a time. We had tremendous support and prayers from our family, relatives, friends, prayer groups, and people we didn't even know. Thank you!

Elly was now up to eight doctors (pediatrician, hematologist, genetics, endocrinologist, neurologist, ophthalmologist, gastroenterologist, nephrologist), surgeons, and a social worker. New medications were also added (see Resource and Definition page). A steroid was added at a later date. Antibiotics were also added when needed. As you can see, her daily routines were extensive. Did we mind? Not at all. We did what we had to do. It is amazing what you can do with the strength of Christ, faith, and love.

Elly's First Birthday

October 1, Elly's first birthday! We celebrated her first birthday in Children's Hospital. Her daddy, her sisters, and I made her first birthday as wonderful and meaningful as we could. We realized that she really wasn't feeling up to this celebration, but we made the best of it. We had balloons, presents, and her very own birthday cake. The nursing staff helped in planning and arranging her party. They were also invited along with the physicians. We had a very nice day. Not only did we celebrate her first birthday, but we celebrated her life!

It was difficult for our family at times, for we weren't together as we would have liked, but our daughters understood. Our family was strong, and we worked to pull life and love together. We were so blessed, for we knew what was needed, and we did it. We respected one another and worked together for the love of Elly. Her sisters did miss school days, but the priest, principal, teachers, and faculty were so very kind and compassionate, for they understood the severity of the situation. They helped us in any way they could. They helped in tutoring our children, sending schoolwork home so we could stay on task for school, and they prayed for Elly and us as well. We truly appreciated them. As for her daddy, he had to stay at home and maintain his business for our financial needs. He came down every chance he could, and he did stretch himself thin. He not only worked his business, but he took care of our other daughters with the help of my parents. He was super daddy. I truly realized and understood that every day of my life I was truly blessed. I have an amazing family.

Now let's get back to Elly's journey. She had numerous blood transfusions. She was admitted to the NICU two more times. She also was in need of a platelet transfusion at one point. With this transfusion, she had a severe reaction. Her blood sugar and blood pressure took a nose-dive! I thanked God that she had a one-on-one nurse with this transfusion. She acted immediately, which diverted a serious reaction into a critical one.

I am urging mothers to never feel intimidated or helpless when it comes to your child's health. When you are in a situation and feel strongly that something is wrong with your child, you need to speak up and make the doctors and nurses listen in any way you can, for you are the mother, and you know your child! God gave us his leading, and by all means listen to that little voice within you. I have had to battle with them many times, but in the end, I won. They finally realized that I did understand this syndrome, and I most certainly understood my daughter's symptoms. I knew what my daughter needed. Finally, when I said there was a problem, they reacted diligently. This did not happen overnight. As a matter of fact, it was a process of earning their respect but yet being true to my daughter's needs. There were many times issues arose, and I never gave up. I was diligent. I never gave up on keeping them up to speed on her condition. Our family fought for Elly. When the doctors and nurses started to listen to what I had to say, it helped keep her out of the NICU. Thank God!

We had another team meeting with all the doctors and the two social workers. This meeting was, once again, to discuss what our next steps would be. Once again, no one knew what to do. My husband and I sat there in amazement, for we thought that if we were able to bring the team of doctors together, that they could discuss and give suggestions around the table coming up with a game plan. It almost seemed that time stood still as we all sat there. So, my husband broke the ice by asking if there was a gene finder, meaning what gene was causing this syndrome and could there be a way to fix this gene. The doctors replied this was not an option, for there were too many genes that were affected. We took another step and asked them, "What about a kidney transplant to help with her Fanconi syndrome?"

Their reply was this: "This is not an option either." We asked about different herbs that may help her. Their reply was "This is not an option either."

So our next question was "Will Elly ever get off of her IV and feeding tubes?"

Answer, "No." With these answers, my husband and I became very upset, for we felt that they had just given up on our daughter, and they were just letting this syndrome take its course. We felt that there was a disconnect, for none of the doctors were talking with the other doctors, discussing the medications that they prescribed or what they were doing in terms of medical necessity. I finally had enough! Trembling, I stood up and pleaded that we work together as a team. Then in anger, I said, "Not one of you in this room knows what the other doctor is doing with our daughter! This isn't an experiment we are were working on. This is our daughter's life at stake." In desperation, I suggested that I would be the team leader again and call all the doctors to inform them of what was going on with Elly.

As you recall, we already had multiple team meetings where Steve and I were the leaders, but as the team had grown, more meetings had needed to be held. I believed that we would *get* further, acting as one team rather than having everyone do their own medical decisions without the others. They suggested that her hematologist be the team leader. Relieved, we agreed. At least, we were getting somewhere. Our meeting had not been as successful as we had hoped, but we knew that we had been heard! A team leader had been designated to take on this precious life task. As you can see, we tried to always look to the positive, but there were times we were angry, upset, frustrated, and even furious. With that said, we knew it was our right to fight for our daughter's life, and the fighting we did, and the fight would continue. Nor did we always settle for their answers. We felt, as parents, there should be more that could be done! We just *knew* there was more. I will never forget a couple of confrontations I had with Elly's doctors. I remember asking one of the doctors questions, and maybe too many at the time, but he was not able to answer any of them. He became upset with me and said, "You need to be quiet and stop asking me so many questions."

I became furious! I felt a rage well up inside of me, and I said to him, as well as everyone else in that room, "You may have forgotten, but this is my daughter, and I will not give up on her as you have. You are looking at the medical aspect of this syndrome, and I am looking at our faith in this very special time of need. I ask that you look at her with compassion and help us help her. Miracles happen every day, as you are aware of, so please do not give up on her nor give up on us!" I knew very well what the odds were and the battle we were facing, but I was so tired of getting my hopes up when our daughter would have wonderful days, only to have the doctor or doctors burst my bubble every time. Yes, I was very much aware that she could die. They would say "she will die." This is where we clashed.

They said she would, and we said she would not. My husband and I prayed and had strong faith in God, while they went by their statistics and medical data. They were scientific, and we were depending on our God. As you can see, it is hard for the scientific arena to step over into supernatural faith. Elly and our family received strength, courage, and knowledge, not only by the medical profession but from God as well. He definitely was there even at times we thought he had deserted us. We were living day by day and cherishing every moment we had together. As parents, you always have faith, hope, and love, for this is the recipe to live each day. We were asking for the doctors to do the same. I don't blame them now, for they had so many patients in their care and could only see the facts, results, and conclusions that lay before them on their desks. It is so very hard to jump from facts to faith, hope, and love. I do understand they become detached for they see many children die. They lose themselves, or should I say their faith has been wounded. I did get them talking, and they *had* seen miracles. So as you see, supernatural events are not lost. As they also came to this realization, I said, "I rest my case." I encouraged them to never give up *but* to believe in what they could not see.

We know better than anyone else that there are struggles in family life; however, aren't they needed to make us stronger? Elly and I were in hospitals most of her life, while my husband worked and our other two beautiful daughters went to school. We tried to live a normal life, but what exactly is a normal life? Elly and I missed our family very much. I knew they were well taken care of. My parents played a very important role in their lives as well as ours. I am so very thankful and grateful for their love, for without them, the struggle would have been unbearable. It tore me apart when Lindsey and Jesi would ask me when we were coming home. When it was possible, we made arrangements for them to stay with us at the hospital. Our situation affected them because they never knew if we would be home when they got home from school or if we would be there when they woke up in the morning. I felt that their security was taken away from them for a short time. They are amazing daughters, and I believe they understood the risk of their sister's condition. They so missed her. So as you can see, family life is put to the test time and time again, but *love* conquers all! I love my husband and children very much. I have been so blessed. As a mother, being torn away from your children is difficult, so I tried with all my being to bring our family together as a whole when possible.

When it came to holidays, we never knew if we would be together or split up between the hospital and home. Every holiday that Elly was home, we celebrated with joy. As a matter of fact, we celebrated every day as if it were a holiday, for Steve and I had been blessed with three beautiful daughters. I remember when Elly was feeling well, they would play together as children play without sickness looming over them. As I mentioned earlier, Elly knew exactly when her sisters and Daddy would arrive home from school and work. She had this uncanny intuition. How did I know? When the time came for them to walk through the door, she would be so excited and would move her body with such joy. She never spoke at this time in her life, but her nonverbal was more accurate and louder than any voice could have shouted with joy!

Elly started to improve on October 18. She adjusted well to her new life with her life-saving tubes. This enabled us to move by ambulance to a hospital closer to home.

She continued her hospitalization for approximately two more weeks. At this hospital, I became completely knowledgeable with the titration process and the pumps. What does this mean? (See Resource and Definition page.) We needed to balance her feeds as well as her electrolytes. If her body could tolerate the fluid levels, then she could be taken off the IV fluids and feeds. However, this will be a long journey. I still was very nervous with the Broviac site and G-J stoma (system). What I was *really* saying was that I was actually petrified of the Broviac site. That was my most fearful site. The nurses in this hospital were becoming comfortable with Elly again, since she had given them such a scare the last time she had been admitted there. Elly became quite close with the nurses, doctors, lab technicians, x-ray staff, cleaning staff, etc. They were all a second family to us! This hospital was our second home, our second family. As our stay was coming to a close, the social worker at this hospital had quite a chore. She had to find in-home nurses. This task was a tough one, for she needed experienced nurses that could deal with *all* of Elly's necessities.

October 31. Elly was discharged! Amazing! We had dreamed of this day when we could go home with our family. Today was Halloween. I was so filled with joy that we could go home and resume our somewhat normal life. Before she was discharged, Elly's nurses had to meet us at the hospital to ride home with us. When we arrived home, we met with another nurse who would stay with us until later that evening. We had to be mindful of shift changes. This was new to us, but we were very grateful. Elly had sixteen hours of nursing care a day. The evening shift nurse, who had been there with us originally, had to quit due to the high-pressure responsibilities. Our home was now an ICU. It was quite hard finding nurses who felt secure and were not afraid of harming her. Eventually, we found nurses that would be a part of our lives. Their skills were put into action immediately. Titrations needed to begin due to frequent vomiting and bowel movements. I watched closely, for I was educating myself. I was amazed at how well I handled the titrations. Now, I was not an expert like the nurses, but I felt comfortable in this process. Keep in mind, mothers know their children.

As you can imagine, our days always passed by quickly. We never had a dull moment. As mentioned prior, our home was now an intensive care unit with all the appropriate supplies at our fingertips.

Every supply had its place. We had the IV pump, feeding pump, medicines, injections, IV bags, feeding bags, bandages, etc. The nurses would come in from 7:00 a.m. to 11:00 p.m. Then my shift began in the evening from 11:00 p.m. to 7:00 a.m. Now as a mother, I didn't sleep much, for I kept a very close eye on all the equipment and made sure my daughter was resting peacefully. A parent will do whatever it takes for their children without thinking about their own needs. Yes, I did become grumpy at times and exhausted, but just knowing we were home as a family and Elly was alive was all I needed to keep going.

Now another situation arises. Having nurses in our home was an adjustment. Not only for our family but for the nurses as well. As a matter of fact, quite a few adjustments had to be made to keep family life as normal as possible. There had to be a give-and-take in a situation like this. Maybe I should say a *lot* of "give" in a situation like this. However, we all knew we had to work together as a team to benefit our daughter's life. The nurses started to feel more at ease once they realized that they could determine quickly when something just was not right with her. We kept a close eye on fluid overload, and if this would happen, we would titrate down.

Please note, the details given prior to this were to give you an understanding, or picture if you will, of how this syndrome operated and to give you a more vivid picture of Elly's life.

Along with Elly's IV fluids and feeds, I also needed so desperately to feed her by mouth. The reason for this was to administer her pancreatic enzyme which was oral only. Along with the pancreatic enzyme, she needed her Coenzyme Q tablet with food as well. This medication also helped with the mitochondrial process as well as with her digestive process. So as you can see, it was imperative that she received these medications. You might think that this was not a great concern. However, on the contrary, it most certainly was. Elly did not eat food. We were not sure of the reason. The only way I was able to get these medications into her system was with her pacifier. She had always enjoyed her pacifier, even since birth. When I would insert food containing crushed medication into her mouth, I would follow it with her pacifier, which enabled her to swallow. She associated her pacifier with sucking and swallowing. So as you can see, the pacifier was a device that aided in her syndrome not only with medications but by keeping her sucking reflex intact. We did experiment with the oral medications through her feeding tube, but that only caused the tube to become clogged, which in turn caused additional problems. You would think, being the problem solvers that we were that this technique was the overall answer. No, it was not. Elly was not able to swallow food all the time. It was only intermittently that she could do so.

Thirteen Months of Age

November 3. Elly was now thirteen pounds, two ounces. She now had a pediatric nurse who would come weekly to assist the home nurses in aid of the Broviac dressing. This dressing had to be changed one time weekly and had to be in a sterile environment, as much as possible, in a home setting. It took two nurses to do this. Elly did not like this task at all. She would become very upset each time, but she knew her mommy was right there to give her cuddles and love after the process was finished. Once the dressing was changed, blood work had to be drawn, which helped to keep a check on her blood and electrolytes. These blood draws became easy now for Elly. She no longer is being pricked or stabbed anymore, for the nurse drew the blood out of her Broviac line. Ten days later, she had gained weight. She was now fourteen pounds, four ounces.

Now Elly was a little tease, and she had such a fun, loving spirit. She would pull and tug at her dressing, tearing it three-fourths of the way off. Of course, this made Mommy and Daddy very uneasy, but she laughed, and we refastened it the best we could. She also tugged at her G-J tube, pulling it out further than we would like. So that had to be adjusted, and we didn't care for that much either. However, inside we were giggling, for she thought she was funny. So Daddy and I came up with a solution, or so we thought. We would put a onesie on her to help prevent her from getting to her tubes. One day she managed to pull the tape that reinforced the bandages. This was the main bandage that held the Broviac line in place, and she had torn out two or three stitches. Thank goodness it was only two or three, but too many for Mommy, for I started to panic. The nurses reassured me that this was okay and that we would have this checked at her next appointment. I calmed down and kept a very close eye on her hands.

November 17. Elly had her blood drawn today. She wasn't feeling all that well. This blood draw would let us know where her complete blood count and electrolytes were, meaning were they within normal limits or is there cause for concern. I was very thankful for the nurses. They were such a help especially when I needed to take my daughter to the doctors or hospitals or to pick up her sisters, etc. It took two people to get her ready and into the van for traveling. The reason it took two people is this. I would get her ready, as well as her diaper bag, and make sure I had her oral medications. The nurse would make sure the pumps were in working order and that we had enough IV solution, along with her feeds. Also, she had to make sure they had supplies such as syringes, bandages, Sprite to unclog tubing, batteries for pumps, and other supplies that may have been needed for that day. As you can see, this was not a one-man job but two.

Now before we would get into the van, we had to take her IV bags and feeding bags and place them in a separate knapsack. All of her medications had to be measured and accounted for along with her time sheet, which kept track of when she would need to take her medications. If the IV solution and feeding bags were not enough to last the trip, we had to take extra, which we placed on ice in another bag. After we were all packed up and ready to go, one of us would put Elly in her car seat and the other one would grab the IV pole and put it into the van. Once that was completed, one of us ran into the house to grab the bags that held the IV solution and feeding bag. We used the knapsacks for the IV and feeds; however, after some time, we realized that this was causing too many air bubbles in her G-J tube line, and it would upset her stomach.

So after we brainstormed, we decided to leave the bags on the IV pole and put it in the van. This made one less step and seemed to work very well for all of us. So now instead of running back and forth from the van to the house and back again, I would grab Elly and the bags, and the nurse would be right behind us with the IV pole. We had some leeway with her lines but not as much as we would have liked. We had to be extremely careful not to pull on her. We still used the knapsacks when we would go shopping but needed to watch the tubes and lines very closely. As you can see, the preparation for any type of a trip, whether long or short, was a challenging process.

Elly relied upon her mommy, and she knew that I was always there for her. I was not only her mommy, but her security, ambulance driver, and whatever else my darling needed, I did it! As mentioned prior to this journey, we live in a rural area out in the country, so when an emergency would arise, the nurse and I would take off with her to the hospital. We always had supplies ready and on standby for these types of occasions. Now remember, the hospital was an hour away, but it was much faster driving her than waiting upon the ambulance and paramedic crew. After all, I had an experienced nurse with us at all times. So, knowing time was of the essence, we'd take off. We didn't have time to sit and wait due to the critical nature of her syndrome. Every second counted. Now please don't misunderstand me, if we needed help along the way, I definitely would have called 911, and they could have met us en route, but that never was the case.

Within six days, Elly had gained four ounces. She had a glucometer to aid with her blood sugar checks. When she would receive blood transfusions, her blood sugar needed to be taken every fifteen minutes within a half hour to an hour, for her blood sugars would always take a nose-dive. The reason for this was, in order for her to be transfused, the IV solution and her feeds, which contained her dextrose (sugar), had to be put on hold for three hours. As the glucose checks would show, this would be too long for her to be off her IV solution and feeds. Not only was her glucose a concern, but now we had to be concerned with her potassium levels as well. Her normal potassium level should be between 3.6 to 5.2. Her levels would range between 7 to 8. Her legs would tremor from time to time along with her arms. When your potassium level is too high or too low, this can affect your muscles. This is what happened to our daughter with her tremors. We had to be very mindful, if potassium affects the muscles, then it can affect the heart, for your heart is a muscle. This was our main concern. Levels had to be monitored closely. In spite of all this, within four days, we found out her weight had increased to fifteen pounds, two ounces! How did we know this? She had a visit with her pediatrician. At this visit, she was diagnosed with a sinus and ear infection. Also, her potassium was high. She was prescribed Vancenase for a congested nose. Vancenase is a nasal spray that sometimes can cause bleeding. This also had to be monitored closely.

Thanksgiving Day! We were able to stay home with our family and enjoy this holiday together. Praise the Lord! We had so much to be thankful for, and we made that known. We went next door to Grandma and Grandpa's house for dinner. We all had a wonderful day together. Our whole family was there, including uncles, aunts, and cousins. We were enjoying life!

The day after Thanksgiving, Elly's bottom was very red and blistered. This would happen from time to time. This was due to acid burns, which were caused by her urine dispensing or producing too much sodium. We had tried many products to help relieve the pain. Some products helped, and some did not. We also had to do mouth care. For other children, brushing teeth is the way to go. However, for Elly we had to use Toothettes soaked in Sprite to swab her mouth. This aided in grabbing and removing the thick mucus that she would produce, to help clear her airway. If we didn't have the Toothettes, we would use lemon glycerin swabs. We also had to make a trip to the emergency room for a recheck on her sinus and ear infection. She needed a Rocephin shot (antibiotic injection), which really worked well for her. At that time, her potassium was rechecked, and it was down to 6.1.

Fourteen Months of Age

December 1. Today was Elly's weekly nurse visit. She weighed fifteen pounds, four ounces. Her potassium level was back up to 7.8. Her blood work was scheduled to be drawn in two days. As I think back, I wanted so much to keep her in a bubble so she would not be subjected to any type of bacteria. I know that was not reality, but what a family won't think of. As a family, we were still trying to live a so-called normal life, but then what is normal? Let me define our normal. As a family, we lived a life that was normal for us. Elly's daddy and sisters washed their hands and changed their clothes immediately when they arrived home from school and work. Anyone outside of our family was not permitted into our home, especially if they were sick or had been exposed to something. Did this cause friction? Yes, a little, but we all knew that it was for the best. Remember our household had become an ICU setting. As a matter of fact, if any of the family were sick, they would stay in a different room. However, Elly did not like that, so we made an alternate plan. We would wear masks. Elly so enjoyed having her family around her. Not only did the family wear masks but so did the nurses, if needed. To keep this family functioning to our normal, anyone who came into our household had to follow the same procedures as we did, including Lindsey's and Jesi's friends. Our goal was to keep our other two daughter's life as stable as possible.

December 5. Elly had just started Viokase, which is another form of the pancreatic enzyme. She had stopped eating altogether.

This medication can be given while her feeds are running. By December 9, she had gained another six ounces. She had also developed a topical staph infection. She had pustules on her skin, which were usually on her face. She was given an antibiotic, along with a new medication called Cortef. This medication was mentioned a while back. Cortef would help aid in the function of her adrenal gland. One of the symptoms of her adrenal gland not functioning properly was that Elly's skin always looked tan.

On December 11, Elly received another blood transfusion. Her bone marrow was not functioning properly. She also had low blood sugar (hypoglycemia). They both create the same symptoms, fatigue and lethargy (weakness), which made it very difficult to distinguish which condition to treat. The next day, she had a stool culture completed, and it came back positive for C-Diff. With this infection, her stools would have a horrendous odor. She wasn't feeling well with both pustules on her skin (staph aureus infection) and now the C-Diff infection. Between the nursing staff and myself, we kept in close contact with the pharmaceutical supply company. Medications were constantly being changed, especially with her IV bags and all other additional supplies. New supplies would come once a week, unless a change had to be made to her IV solution. If this needed changed, they would get it to us speedily. If we would have any trouble with the pumps, a carrier would be sent out immediately, and we would receive it that same day. They were wonderful people, and I appreciated them very much, more than words can say.

Elly would meet with her motor skill therapist (teacher) once a week. She looked forward to these sessions. She was always so excited to see her and to see what she had brought in her bag that day. She enjoyed playing with her. The teacher was helping her develop her gross motor and fine motor skills. They were working on crawling and using sign language.

On December 19, Elly gave up her pacifier. This was not a good sign, for we needed her to keep sucking to keep her reflex strong. What were we going to do? I wondered. We decided that all we could do was to keep moving forward and take care of whatever came our way. And that is what we did.

I am going to give you a picture of our everyday events: We bathed Elly. We changed the Leur lock on the Broviac line, and we changed the Broviac dressing weekly. The nurse changed the stoma dressing daily along with the kangaroo tubing (which was her feeding tube). The teacher visited one time weekly. The pediatric nurse would come one to four times a week to draw blood. We kept a record of Elly's intake and output concerning vomiting and bowel movements. We changed IV batteries and changed IV bags and tubing. We kept track of the inventory and supplies, cleaned pumps, and cleaned toys. We had doctor appointments anywhere from one time a week up to five times a week. With this picture, you're probably wondering when we had time to play. Oh don't worry, we most certainly did play and snuggle. We sang and danced. We read books and rocked. We always found time for fun.

Christmas Eve and Christmas Day, Elly had a wonderful Christmas! We were all so excited, for this was her very first Christmas home with her family. We celebrated by going to Christmas Eve Mass. After church, we visited her great-grandparents for a short while and then off to see her grandparents. Elly enjoyed opening up Christmas gifts. Her eyes lit up when she saw the lights and decorations on the Christmas tree. She was just amazed at all the beauty that surrounded her. She also enjoyed watching her sisters open their Christmas gifts too. She giggled! We came home early and went to bed to await Santa Claus's coming. Her sisters were anxiously waiting for her to wake up so they all could see what Santa had brought them. She finally awoke! It seemed as though it took her forever to wake up, for I believe her family was more excited about Santa Claus coming than she was.

Upon awakening that morning, she had a low-grade fever and had some hoarseness to her voice. She wasn't feeling very well, but she certainly enjoyed Christmas. She was taken into the living room to see what Santa had brought her and her sisters under the tree. She became very excited. It took her all morning to open up her gifts. It most certainly didn't take her sisters that long. We enjoyed our Christmas, for we shared this special time together, and that is of the utmost importance to us. Santa had brought us a very special gift, and that was *time*.

You see, it wasn't the material things that we received that was important, but it was the love that we all shared together, and it was the time we had to do so. Elly gave us her love. The day after Christmas, she had a doctor's appointment. Oh my goodness, she had another sinus and ear infection! Once again, antibiotics were given. She was now up to sixteen pounds, one ounce. Yippee! Four days after Christmas, the mucous in her throat and mouth became so thick that she started choking. She was not able to breathe. Thank God I was able to clear her throat with a Toothette! Her fever was also rising. The next day, we took off to visit her pediatrician's office, for her symptoms were worsening. She had more blood work done. We went back home and awaited the results.

On the morning of New Year's Eve, we received a telephone call from her pediatrician stating that Elly needed to be admitted to the hospital for sepsis. Sepsis is a bacterial infection of the blood. This is very serious and could be a fatal infection depending on the gram rods. What I mean about the rods is there are positive rods and negative rods. Negative rods produce a toxin in the blood that is very deadly. We were notified that Elly had positive rods. Thank God! We asked if we could keep her at home with the nurses, but that idea was rejected, and off to the hospital we went!

That night we spent New Year's Eve together in the hospital. The doctors and nurses expected to see a very sick little girl; however, to their amazement, she was acting as though there was nothing wrong. They couldn't understand this. She even ate crackers and drank from a sippy cup. She never did that before! My husband and I were astounded ourselves and thrilled to life! What more could we ask for? I believe this was a miracle. To be honest, I know it was a miracle. As Elly ate her cracker and drank from her sippy cup, Steve, Lindsey, Jesi, myself, and the nurses on staff shared in shrimp cocktail, pizza, and pop. We were bringing in the new year with joy! As you know, this hospital and these wonderful people were our second home and family. Yes, we were blessed. We had a hospital stay of four days. In this time frame, Elly turned fifteen months of age in the hospital on January 1, 1998.

A side note of fear: The doctors were very concerned, for Elly had been on antibiotics on a regular basis, and they were worried that she would build up an immunity to them and that these antibiotics would not fight the infections as they once had. As they shared their concerns with us, we did what we always did. We listened, and then we prayed. We took one day at a time.

Fifteen Months of Age

On January 12, 1998, we noticed that Elly had four molars coming in. *Wow*! Her teeth were coming in nicely. She hadn't gained any weight; however, she was maintaining it. Even though she was cutting teeth, she was still giving us lots of hugs and kisses, lots of smiles and giggles, and she was just cuddling with her family. She was in a teasing mood. How did we know this? She had this one particular look, smile if you will. We never knew what she was going to do next. She was on the move. How was she on the move? you may ask. She wasn't crawling, but she was scooting on her bottom. She found another way to explore her environment. She was so adorable moving this way and she giggled.

January 21, Elly weighed seventeen pounds. This was the most she had ever weighed! We were very pleased. In four days, she had gained four more ounces. However, today, she had another low-grade fever indicating a problem. Before this, we needed to watch for acidosis and dehydration. Now we would also need to keep a close eye on fevers and infections. The next day, her potassium was 7.2 and her platelets were low. A couple of days later, she had pustules around her G-J stoma, accompanied by another low-grade fever. A culture was completed on the drainage and on the pustules along with blood work. The culture and blood work indicated that she had another infection (staph aureus) requiring another antibiotic.

Sixteen Months of Age

February 1. Steve, Elly, the nurse, and I made a trip to Children's Hospital. We had an appointment with a nutritionist on how to get her to eat. Her eyes were very photophobic today. Also, she had a new G-J tube placed today by radiology. We also visited with her hematologist and had more blood work completed. We visited with her gastroenterologist, and we received more medication changes on her Propulsid and Viokase. A stool sample was taken for C-Diff. C-Diff is caused by taking too many antibiotics. We then visited her endocrinologist. All doctors would notify us of the results of the tests that were completed. It was reassuring, and very considerate, that they would schedule all of Elly's appointments on the same day to limit travel time, since that was the hospital that was three hours away.

February 4. Elly had an appointment with her pediatrician. A CBC, electrolytes, stool culture, nose and throat cultures, and x-rays were ordered. She was weighing in today at seventeen pounds, fourteen ounces. She was extremely photophobic, so she was not able to handle any type of light. We sat in the dark that day to help eliminate discomfort. We received the results of Elly's tests, and she was septic again. We were able to stay at home this time, for her pediatrician and I felt that she would be better cared for at home and not subjected to other germs and bacteria. The nurse and I monitored her closely; she had a fever, she was lethargic, and she was limp. The pediatrician changed her antibiotic. A problem occurred with our home nurse, for she was uncomfortable with Elly being treated at home. This caused some friction between us, for I agreed with the doctor that Elly would be subjected to less germs at home.

Elly's pediatrician admitted her into the hospital on February 6. Was I upset? Yes. Did I understand? Yes. Did I like it? No. The nurses couldn't understand that I knew when my daughter was in trouble. I was her mother after all! I had proved that to Elly's pediatrician, and he trusted me. However, our hands were tied when the nurse spoke up and said that she was uncomfortable, for she was concerned that this could cause issues in Elly's care. Would I have let that happen? Absolutely not! However, I had to keep in mind that they were human, and they were frightened of this syndrome. I knew they had Elly's best interest at heart as we all did. This helped me to keep things in perspective. Now keep in mind, there was never an easy path when it came to the nurses. Some would quit, some were fired, and some were just plain terrified of her symptoms. My goodness! When I started out, I was too, but I couldn't understand why they had a hard time trusting my judgment.

So, Elly and I loaded up with all the equipment and supplies, picked my mom up from her work, and off we went. I remembered being so nervous and upset, for I always had a nurse to aid Elly in the back of the van while I was driving. Elly who was used to having a nurse ride beside her was crying and so upset too. I stopped frequently to calm Elly, so it took me a while to reach my mom who now rode beside her. I was terrified to have her ride in the back by herself for many reasons, as I've mentioned throughout this journey. We made it to the hospital without complications. I believe in prayer!

February 9. Elly was discharged with an IV antibiotic for ten days. She had lost approximately three ounces. She was still vomiting every day. On February 13, I took part in administering Elly's IV antibiotics. Once again, I was extremely nervous, and I might add terrified, but I had no choice. It was amazing what you find yourself doing when it comes to your children. I'd either end the antibiotic or I would do both from start to finish. This antibiotic may not be started until 12:00 a.m. and finish at 2:00 a.m. It wasn't difficult. Everything needed to be sterile, and her Broviac line needed to be flushed before and after her antibiotic was administered. The reason for the flushing was due to the antibiotic and the IV solution being incompatible. In other words, they were not able to be mixed together. It sure was easier with two people, but when I was alone, fear consumed me. I certainly needed to be in the know. I was extremely cautious. This was my choice, for this was my daughter's life, and of course, I will do anything in this world to keep her healthy. I would do this for any of my daughters.

On February 24, Elly had an appointment with her pediatrician, and all was well. In just a few days, we had another appointment with her pediatrician, and now she had a fever of 102 degrees, which was taken under her arm. Her potassium was very high again, and she had pustules on her forehead and her eye. Elly had another infection, which was treated, and her IV solution was changed.

February 28. Elly had an episode today. She was having an extremely hard time breathing and was wheezing terribly. Her breathing was very heavy at times. She turned blue at one point. She was acting different from other times, and her eyes were glassy. I told the nurse that we needed to go to the ER *now*! Elly had been admitted by her pediatrician's associate for observation, because by the time we reached the ER, she had come back around.

Seventeen Months of Age

March 1. Prior to Elly being discharged today, a blood transfusion was ordered due to the result of her blood count. As she was being transfused, her blood sugar dropped dramatically, and she started to shake uncontrollably with a temperature of 102.9. The blood transfusion was stopped immediately. Within that time, her temperature had increased to 103.6. Elly was not discharged after all, and so our family and the nurse went home without us. As it turned out, Elly was septic again. I prayed all day, asking God to watch over her and protect her. She was discharged in March 6.

She was weighed the next day, and she weighed eighteen pounds, four ounces. We were so very excited! Her blood cultures showed a staph infection, so we needed to monitor that by keeping an eye on her temperature. We were told, if it would start to climb, we would need to rush her to Children's Hospital. The doctor felt that the IV tubing may be holding bacteria and may need to be changed. By March 10, she had become listless. She was having nosebleeds, and she was hoarse. More blood work was completed, and no infection was identified! This is good. We did not have to make a trip to the Children's Hospital. She was started on a new antibiotic. I was in high hopes that the home nurse would stay and help monitor her; however, this was not possible, for her shift had ended.

When the antibiotic would come in a self-timing canister, I had no problem administering it. I would become uncomfortable when it had to be administered through the IV bag. Just the same, I managed just fine. With the self-timing canisters, all I had to do was flush the line before and after and hook her back up to her IV solution. These canisters were very helpful and unique. Nothing needed to be handled or inserted. It was a ready-to-go medicine. On this particular day, I hooked up Elly's antibiotic canister; then, she and I took a nap while it infused. When I awoke, to my horror, Elly was drenched in blood! The bedsheets were soaked! The comforter was soaked! I called out to the nurse immediately! As it turned out, the canister that was infusing her antibiotic had been cracked undetectably, allowing Elly's blood to run out of the tubing. This antibiotic was connected for thirty minutes, but when the actual episode took place, we do not know. Thank God that her blood clotted! Her blood is so very precious!

Nevertheless, it was too long for Elly, for we had no idea how much blood she lost, but we did know it was a considerable amount. Every drop of her blood was essential to her. I was almost positive that she would need another blood transfusion in the very near future. Now the next major concern would be this: whether or not her blood had clotted *too* much, rendering her Broviac line unusable. The nurse tried to flush the line with no success. When she started to flush the line, a huge bubble would appear indicating clogging in the tube. The first problem was that we could not disconnect the canister from her line. It was like it was suctioned to it. After many attempts, we finally succeeded in disconnecting it. We also used heparin to try to unclog the tubing, but this action was also unsuccessful. Needless to say, we were off to the ER to see if the doctor could thin her blood enough to start the blood flowing again.

At the hospital, a medicine was given, which acted like heparin but was much stronger. This medicine was called urokinase. This medicine was very dangerous to Elly, because her platelets were low. Thinning her blood too much could result in a hemorrhage. It took the doctor three attempts to unclog the tubing. Between each attempt, there had to be a one-hour interval. I was so relieved, for if it wasn't successful, we would have had to go back to Children's Hospital for surgery to put in a new line. Blood cultures were now necessary, for with her line being open, she was at a higher risk for infection. No infection indicated!

Elly was always behind on her immunizations due to her syndrome. However, on March 18, she had an appointment with her pediatrician to receive a set of them. At that time, a nose culture was completed to make sure there was no staph infection. We also wanted to see why Elly's nose would bleed when she sneezed.

Good news! She weighs nineteen pounds today! Hooray! The next couple of days were uneventful. Super!

I can't express this enough. Even though we have had many trials and tribulations, we also had many joys in our lives. I don't want you to think that we focused on the negativity. Our family, with whom I had been truly blessed, had been given many opportunities for extreme joy, in good times and in bad. We embraced every one of those opportunities with gratitude.

Now with that said, we had another concern pop up that I hadn't even thought of before. This concern involved the insurance company. The questions that arose were about the nurses. Which nurses did Elly actually need for her explicit care? Which ones did the insurance company feel were not necessary for Elly's care? As you recall, Elly had a pediatric nurse come in one to four times a week to draw blood and change her Broviac dressing. As I spoke with the insurance company, they stated that two different nursing facilities were not necessary in my daughter's care. Hmm, I thought to myself. As I recall, I asked the person I was speaking to if they had a medical background and what qualified them to make this call. This person, however, was following policy and protocol, and of course, they had to adhere to that. I had a very hard time with this. So, did I fight this? Absolutely! However, until I was able to work with the insurance company and doctor, I had to follow their protocols. This was a major problem, and I will explain the reasons.

They stated there was no need for a professional and skilled nursing facility in our home. Well, what did they know about my daughter's condition? Nothing. How could they, when the rest of us were trying to deal with a condition that was so rare. They wanted Elly and I to go to the hospital for blood draws. The closest hospital was thirty minutes away, and they were not at all familiar with her case. To comply with the insurance company, I took her to this hospital for a period. This hospital staff was curious in Elly's case and wanted to draw blood for their own purposes. That was stopped immediately. We already had a team who was familiar with her condition, and that was who would deal with her condition. Involving inexperienced staff in Elly's care would be a health risk. Not only would that have been a health risk, but exposing her to more germs and bacteria on an almost daily basis would not have benefitted Elly in the least.

The other solution would have been for me to run the blood to the nearest hospital. However, this would have been impossible. Why? Because of the resulting complications. Elly was very dependent upon my presence whether the nurses were there or not. If I were to leave, this would cause Elly to cry. Remember reading awhile back that when Elly would cry, the risk could increase for her to become acidotic, and it could throw off her electrolytes? This creates a dangerous situation for her, so I refused this option. Steve's and my main concern was not what was best for us or others but what was best for Elly! Keep in mind both options were a health risk, so we couldn't go with either of them.

It was suggested that the skilled nurses draw her blood from the Broviac line. That may have worked, had they had enough experience in this field. However, they did not, and I might add that they were frightened to work with her Broviac as well. I understood their feelings, and I would not ask them to do this if they were not comfortable. You see, they were not NICU nurses. The pediatric nurse that came in to see Elly and to do the NICU tasks was experienced in this field. I might add that she was an exceptional nurse, not only with Elly but with our family as well. While our battle was still in progress, Elly, the skilled nurse, and I would run to the hospital to have her blood drawn. This was not a good scenario, but we didn't have any other choice at this time. We were still fighting for the skilled and professional nurses to stay in-home.

I spoke with Elly's pediatrician, and he took matters into his own hands. He called the insurance company and explained in complete detail the condition and health risks that are at stake. He also stated that our home was now a NICU setting and that the family needed to keep all staff on board! The insurance company finally agreed to have both facilities in the home. Thank you, Jesus!

Eighteen Months of Age

On April 1, Elly turned eighteen months of age. On April 2, pustules were noted on her neck. Gentamycin ointment was prescribed to treat them. She weighed nineteen pounds and one and a half ounces. I spoke with her pediatrician regarding her G-J tube. I explained that it would hurt her belly terribly when medications were administered and that it was hard to push the medications through the tube. I explained that we met resistance. He stated that the placement of her G-J tube would need to be checked by using the barium method. This was done, and the test resulted in a positive result. Her tube placement was correct, and no further action needed to be done. No additional surgery was needed to correct the tube. However, more blood cultures were taken. Days passed, and we lived and enjoyed our normal life. I remember Elly and her sisters playing on the waterbed, going for walks, reading, watching movies, playing with toys, eating together as a family, and going to church together. Family matters!

In the early morning of April 18, approximately 2:00 a.m., I noticed a blood return in Elly's antibiotic canister. I stayed up the rest of the night keeping a very close eye on this. I was very concerned and wondered why this would be happening and what might come of it. It took a while for the blood to disappear into her Broviac line. The nurse arrived at 8:00 a.m., and I told her right away of the incident. She looked at the line, and everything was good. The line flushed well. However, keep in mind the antibiotic was already administered, and the IV solution was hooked back up. I just wanted the nurse to be aware of the situation. Elly's morning went very well up until approximately 12:30 p.m. While I was rocking her, I felt something wet. I looked down and to my horror found Elly's blood all over my shirt and pants. Elly's outfit was soaked in the front with her blood!

I yelled for the nurse to come quickly. The nurse found a crack in the Broviac tubing causing the back blood flow earlier that morning and causing the leakage this early afternoon. The nurse cleaned the area extremely well and clamped off the tubing above the crack to prevent further leakage. The nurse called the hospital to find a doctor who could mend this, but there wasn't one available at that time. The nurse mended it just long enough for Elly, Lindsey, Jesi, the nurse, and I to make a quick trip to Children's Hospital. Elly had lost a lot of blood again, and the risk for infection was now another concern. At Children's Hospital, they were able to repair it. This saved Elly again from needing surgery. It took quite a while to repair it, and urokinase was used again to unclog the tubing. It was a success! We returned home at approximately 11:30 p.m.

On April 20, Elly needed another blood transfusion. The next day was her sister Lindsey's birthday. Elly was so excited when we celebrated her birthday. There were balloons, a pirate cake, and presents. Elly so enjoyed watching everyone and joining in the festivities. Her laugh was contagious! The next few days, she was learning and beginning to shake her head "yes" and "no." She was communicating with us and answering our questions! This was a major step in her development! She pointed to what she wanted. She lifted and held her arms out to be held. She scooted on her butt to get where she wanted to go, as she explored her environment. She was also using simple sign language to get her needs met. She was a very smart little girl!

Approximately one week later, Elly cries every time she would urinate due to the acid burns on her bottom area. This was extremely painful for her.

Nineteen Months of Age

May 1. Elly was beginning to get up on her hands and knees and would rock a little. She would go from a crawling position to a sitting position. We were very hopeful she would start crawling soon. We had no worries, for Elly always managed to scoot to where she wanted to go. "Where there is a will, there is a way." We were so proud of her progress! She also enjoyed certain activities, such as playing in her activity chair and watching *Teletubbies* and *Blues Clues*, and she was always on the move and playing. She felt free. Thank goodness her lines were long enough to keep up with her. We only had to make sure we moved her IV and feeding pole with her. All the times we spent together were a blessing.

By the following day, May 2, Elly had lost a little weight. We were not happy with this. Today and every day we would clean the G-J tube and put a new dressing on it. Sometimes her site would be infected and sometimes not. The next day, she came down with a low-grade fever, and her eyes were bothering her again. Her lips were cracked and bleeding; however, Blistex helped with this. She was also experiencing drainage from her G-J tube. At certain times, her medications would meet resistance when given. We were holding off on her medications and feeds until her belly would settle down and the bloating would decrease; then, we would resume them.

On May 3, Elly weighed nineteen pounds, six ounces with her clothes on. We made a trip to Children's Hospital to meet with all her doctors. The gastroenterologist increased her Viokase, and her Peptamin Jr. was replaced with Neocate Plus, which was a new type of food. Also her G-J tube was replaced. Her endocrinologist increased her Cortef. Her hematologist completed and received her blood draw results. Genetics saw Elly and were surprised at how well she was doing. She was growing nicely, physically and developmentally. They felt that her hair was very light blonde due to the mitochondria syndrome until I explained to them that her sisters also had very light blond hair when they were her age. When Elly was born, she had very dark brown hair, and as time went on, she lost her hair, and it came in a very light blonde color.

That day, our visit went well. Our trip home went very well too. Elly was worn out, for she had experienced a very busy day. As for Steve and I, we were just mind boggled, trying to absorb all the information and medication changes that were given to us today. We always took notes and asked a lot of questions. When we got home, we would always review the information.

May 5. Elly had lost a little more weight. She was now nineteen pounds, two ounces. She was unable to open her eyes that morning due to severe photophobia. Also, she had a fever, and her lips were cracked and bleeding. She was in her high chair with pudding and carrots on her tray when she offered me some of her food; however, *she* never tried it. We always encouraged Elly to take a bite on her own. Her belly was hurting, and she was vomiting thick yellow mucous with yellow bile this day as well. By the next day, her fever was gone.

Elly was playing tricks on her mommy and nurse today. She would bring her bowl to her mouth, which made the nurse and me cheer, and we would clap. Then she would laugh and do it again. She repeated this action many times; unfortunately, she never took a bite. There was milk in her sippy cup, and she would put the cup to her mouth, take a drink, and spit it out. I was so happy, for she was improving on her feeding skills. Did she eat? No, but she was making steps toward this motion. We had a wonderful day today!

The next day, May 7, she was vomiting quite a bit in the morning. She wasn't having a very good day today. A urine sample needed to be obtained. We took her to the lab to give a urine sample. That afternoon, she became fussier. The nurse got her to eat ice cream by herself! She loved it, and I was overjoyed! Stoma drainage was apparent, so her dressing needed to be changed quite frequently. The drainage was the color of yellow bile. She held her own for the next few days.

On May 14, Elly was having a nice day, nothing out of the ordinary. By 11:00 p.m., she started to shake uncontrollably. Her fever was rising, and her breathing was very fast. Her breathing was very unusual, because she was breathing with really quick breaths and very hard. Deep down inside, I was aware of a dreadful panic. These symptoms were different. She had never acted like this before. I notified her pediatrician immediately. He felt that she was hyperventilating. He said if she was not better in a half hour to an hour to bring her to the ER. Steve cuddled her so tenderly and sweetly, and she calmed down. I thanked God for her daddy, for he was always the calm, tender-hearted one. I thank God for him even to this day! My inner being still knew that she was in some sort of trouble, but she settled right down and went back to acting like herself. This was very unusual!

The next day, May 15, Elly had a *fabulous* day. I mean *extraordinary*! She was playing and laughing. As I watched from the window, she played outside with her daddy and was *not* photophobic. This day was a bright day of sunshine. Elly watched and pointed to a butterfly in complete wonder. She was so fascinated by this. She explored the outside like she never did before! The whole day was magical. It was a beautiful day, just as she was, beaming in that day light! When she laughed, she made a little snoot face and produced a joyful noise. The snoot face, as described prior, was when she crinkled her nose and smiled. She had the *best* day ever. What a *joy*! Today I was so filled with happiness, hope, and love. It was a *splendid* day! As this day went on, I thought back to how I had overreacted to her hyperventilating. I said to myself, "See, everything is fine, for she is having the time of her life." Our family was on cloud nine! Her sisters were now outside with her and their daddy. As I gazed upon my family, I saw such love and joy, and I saw a normal family living life. Later that evening, she started to run a low-grade fever. *Oh God*!

The next day, May 16, Elly still had a low-grade fever, and she was not tolerating her feeds at all. We turned them off, and she was strictly on her IV fluids. The doctor on call was notified. Saturday, May 17, Elly didn't seem herself in the morning. All she wanted to do was rock. I always enjoyed rocking with her. Later that morning, she had the same hyperventilating experience she had on Thursday night. Then by noon, she was playing and happy again. She had stopped vomiting. She was rolling around and went from a crawling position to a sitting position by herself. She was in a wonderful mood. At 3:00 p.m., before her nap time, her temperature was 98.6. She had a good nap, but when she awoke, she became fussy again. Her temperature spiked to 103.9. The nurse, my mom, Lindsey, Jesi, and I rushed her to the ER. Steve and my dad followed behind. Within half an hour, her temperature became even higher. When we reached the ER, Elly was having difficulty breathing. Blood cultures were taken along with a CBC workup. Life flight was called in to transport her to Children's Hospital. I remember that day as though it was yesterday. The events that took place were beyond comprehension! That night was very stormy, so the life flight crew was unable to come right away. It seemed an eternity before they actually arrived. It was so windy, and there was lightning flashing everywhere. The next step would have been to transport her by ambulance, for they felt they had no other choice. They needed to get her to Children's Hospital as soon as possible. Precious time was passing, and with each moment, she was becoming worse. For as sick as our "love bug" was, she still motioned for her mommy and daddy to cuddle her. Her hand was so weak but very innocent and sweet. The doctor on call said, "For as sick as she is, it must be a miracle, for she is still alive and active." I was becoming very emotional and very anxious inside wondering where the ambulance was.

Between 1:00 to 2:00 a.m., Elly was intubated and flown by helicopter to Children's Hospital. Once again, I was not able to fly with the crew, for they had the maximum weight on board. My heart was crushed. I had never felt such a heaviness before. Once again, my husband and I turned to *God*! I asked God to please watch over and protect her and to make sure their flight was safe. I also remember asking Him to help her, for I knew she needed Him more than ever. She needed Him right now! My husband and I left as soon as we heard *they* were leaving. My mom and dad took our other two daughters home with them. That night was foggy but very still, after the storms went through. During our ride to the hospital, I remember feeling very numb, and I prayed in silence. As for my husband, he had a very difficult drive. He was keeping himself together, but he also had to contend with a fog that was as thick as pea soup. He knew he had to get us there safely, not only for us, but for our daughter. We arrived half an hour before Elly did. My husband had driven very fast. We were two hours away from Children's Hospital. We were on pins and needles awaiting our daughter's arrival. It was a long half hour! In my mind, I kept hoping and praying that this was just another obstacle that we would overcome. Just another bump in the road. Elly arrived and was admitted to the NICU. The days ran into nights. This was one big nightmare we could not seem to wake up from.

Sunday, May 17, Elly was diagnosed with sepsis. She was listed as critical. These words were not only horrifying to me, but my inner being would not give me peace. Please remember that sepsis has two kinds of gram rods. There is a positive rod and a negative rod. This means there are two types of severity. Elly had been diagnosed with this before, but it had always been with the positive gram rod. Today she was diagnosed with the negative gram rod. I wasn't quite sure what all this meant. I asked a lot of questions. The negative gram rod means that once the infection is finally cleared up, it will release toxins into the bloodstream. This makes the battle more difficult. Children and adults do make it through this type of sepsis; it is just a harder battle to conquer. As her daddy and I observed our daughter fighting for her life, I knew she wasn't able to fight *this* time as well as I had prayed and hoped for. Between her daddy and me, we were always right beside her. I would read her stories, sing to her, and hold her precious little hand the whole time. I wasn't able to hold her as I would have liked because she was hooked up to so many different machines. She had a one-on-one nurse, who was exceptional.

Monday, May 18, Elly was still on the respirator. We were hoping to wean her off it yesterday, but no luck. They put her on kidney dialysis that day, hoping to clean her blood and lower her lactic acid, which was 38. Remember, lactic acid's normal count should be 2. Elly was kept under sedation so she wouldn't fight the respirator. She was never awake again from the time she was life flighted.

I want to clarify something here. I believe in prayer. I believe in God the Father. I believe prayer is powerful. From the time Elly was diagnosed, my husband prayed with a group of ladies from our church every morning before he went to work. They were amazing ladies who not only prayed for Elly and our family, but they kept my husband close to their hearts. We needed them now more than ever. We needed everyone's prayers! I would like everyone to know that my husband is a wonderful, caring, and loving man and father!

Tuesday, May 19, Elly was given a blood transfusion, a platelet transfusion, and other blood substances were also given this day. Ever since she had arrived, these transfusions were given at one point or another. I remember a day when she received two blood transfusions. Today was a day unlike the others! Elly bled from her nose! I cried and begged the nurse to do something for her. I pleaded for her to contact the doctors immediately. I was just trembling. I had this feeling of complete helplessness. They didn't seem to be as worried about this situation as I was. I remember calling my cousin, and I just broke down and cried, telling her that Elly wasn't doing very well, and I was so afraid for her life. I kept the heart beat of Elly's love with me at all times, for every one of her heart beats was so very precious! Life is so very precious. I never stopped talking with Elly. I knew she heard her daddy and me talking with her. We were right by her side, and we never gave up! We kept reading stories to her, talking to her, and watching TV with her. We explained to her what was happening on TV and what was funny. We prayed together. We wanted her to know and feel our presence and to know that she was never alone. The only times that we weren't allowed in with her was when there was a crisis going on or when the staff was changing shifts. There were also times when none of these things were going on, and they still told us to leave. They wouldn't let us back in until whatever was happening was resolved. That bothered us, for we were so frightened that it was our daughter they were working on.

Wednesday, May 20. There was still no improvement, but we still did not lose our faith and our heart beat of hope and love. Today Elly seemed a little worse. I had a very uneasy feeling all day. I just couldn't shake it. Steve and I did what we have done all the other days. We were with our baby! Steve and I took a break and went to the Toys R Us store to buy Elly and her sisters stuffed Teletubbies. Elly so enjoyed this show! We went with two of our closest friends; however, it took major persuasion on their part! We knew Elly was in the best care, so we left for a bit, but not long mind you. When we came back, we were so excited to give her the little red Teletubby called Po, and our other two daughters would receive Dipsey who was green and La who was yellow. I kept pushing Po's tummy, and it would talk to Elly. We just wanted Elly to know what we had bought for her, and we hoped it would brighten up her day. Later that day, Elly's uncle, aunt, cousin, and sisters came down to see her. We were so happy. Lindsey and Jesi were also happy with their Teletubbies.

After our family left, the nurse staff was changing shifts, and as always, we were asked to leave. So, my husband and I decided to go grab a bite to eat in the cafeteria. I don't believe we had eaten much during this whole time. We weren't thinking about ourselves of course, and like I said, days ran into nights. As we were eating, a tremendous feeling of fear enveloped me. I became very uneasy. I could not wait for our food to be served, so we could get back to Elly. I needed to get back to her as soon as possible! I remember I lost my appetite. I told my husband that we needed to go *now*! I knew that Elly needed us! We headed straight to the ICU as always, but tonight the doctor met us inside the doorway. Our hearts crashed! We felt numb for we knew this was going to be bad news. Our worst fear! The words that we had never wanted to hear were right now becoming our reality. The doctor took us into a different room and explained to us that Elly had hemorrhaged inside her head, which had pushed her brain into the left side of her head. They showed us the x-rays. I could not comprehend that this was her head, and I couldn't comprehend what I was looking at. They kept talking and pointing and showing us the hemorrhage of her brain, but I couldn't see what they were trying to show us or tell us. I remember that I kept asking, "Which one, which one?" I was not able to understand, because of the state of panic I was in. We pleaded with them to do surgery, saying, "Do whatever it takes, but whatever you do, *help her*!" They explained that if they could, and it would make a difference, they would. But unfortunately, it was too late. Elly was now with God.

My husband and I were allowed to go back to see her. She looked so angelic lying there that it didn't seem possible that what the doctors told us was true. As tears streamed down our faces in disbelief, the nurse showed us Elly's pupils. One pupil was dilated while the other was constricted. I still could not truly comprehend what was happening. I almost felt my body shut down. All I could do was hold her hand, stroke her hair, kiss her, and tell her I love her. I was not able to hold her, for of all the equipment that she was connected to.

The next step was to move her to a private room. I remember seeing families going into this room, but I had never seen any family members coming out of that room with a smile. I had only seen sadness and tears. I remember saying to myself, "That must be the grieving room." Why I had even thought that or said that, I do not know. I prayed that we would never ever have to go into that room. Well, it was just like I imagined it. This room was very private. This room was for the family to be alone with their dying child to say their good-byes. Before our actual move, the nurse asked me what church we belonged to. She asked me who was our priest and what funeral home should they contact. I was unable to answer them, for I could not *remember* our church *or* our priest, so then how could I even *think* of a funeral home? I can't remember if I gave the nurse the church's name or the priest's name. All I do remember is that a very sweet and beautiful minister came to our need. Our family was notified. My mom and dad brought Lindsey and Jesi down so they all could say their goodbyes. Or shall I say "until we meet again in heaven." Two of Elly's uncles were there along with one aunt. Their support at this time was tremendous and greatly appreciated. We so desperately needed their love and support, which they so graciously gave. I will be forever grateful and thankful for their love and compassion. We all prayed together.

They ran a couple of tests on our daughter to see if she had any brain activity. The doctor and nurse took cold water and trickled it on her ears, no response. They did a reflex test, no response. They put water into her eyes and nose with no response. It took all the power I had in me to watch them run these tests, as it did my husband. The sense of helplessness was so overwhelming. We loved her so much, and to see her dying before our eyes was too much to bear. The doctors came into do more testing, and as before, no response. This was too much hurt for one family to withstand. I remember asking God, "If this is your will, take our baby home and take her home now so she doesn't suffer anymore." After I was done talking with God, my husband and I at the same time in one accord shouted, "Please take Elly off the respirator!" Now understand, Steve was at one end of the room, and I was at the other end. We didn't discuss this; we just knew it was time for our baby to go home with Jesus. This decision was made out of pure love and unselfishness.

We wanted more than anything in the world for her to go home with us, but we could not stand to see her go through any more tests and trials. We knew her suffering would cease. We knew without a doubt this was her time. I did pray for a miracle that she would wake up healed, healthy, and alive. But what is a miracle? Miracles come in all kinds of blessings—they come in little nonchalant ways, they come through strangers, and they come through deeds. When you look around and take notice, miracles are happening everywhere in every way. The miracle that did arise was after our prayers. When Elly was disconnected from the respirator, I felt such a presence that I cannot put into words. I felt peace and love in this room. I felt a bright and warm light that was hugging us but with the eye one could not see. This light was so powerful and warm but too incredible to explain. If this makes sense in any way, I knew that we were not alone!

As Elly was taken off the respirator, I was finally able to hold my baby for the first time in days. She felt so wonderful, and she looked so peaceful. As you recall, I had held my daughter daily. So naturally, not being able to do so had given me such emptiness inside. It felt amazing to hold my daughter again. I didn't want to give her up, but with all the strength I could muster, I gave her to her daddy so he could have that last intimate and loving time with her. I remember that even her grandpa held her to say his last goodbye. After her grandpa's goodbye, my husband and I held Elly until her very last heart beat, until her very last breath. As we rocked Elly together, side by side, and while she was lying on her daddy, I felt an amazingly warm touch. It felt as though something was holding us, hugging us, if you will. At one point, for one brief moment, I felt complete comfort, peace, and love in this time of sorrow. At that moment, Elly's spirit was released to go to heaven, her ultimate home…without us. I firmly believe that Jesus was in the room with us. I believe He was hugging us. Her journey had ended here on earth, but her love remains.

When the doctor came in to examine her, Elly's heart was beating no longer. I held her for a little while longer, for I could not bear the thought of leaving her body alone in the hospital. I could not bear the thought of going home without her. I could not bear the thought of never seeing her beautiful face or touching her ever again. I could not bear!

As my husband and I were walking back to the waiting room, I realized that the ICU doctor was walking right behind us. He had tears streaming down his face, for his sorrow and compassion was pure. He gave us his sympathies, and we gave him a hug and thanked him. I thanked him for all the effort he had put forth to try to save our daughter. I knew deep within my heart that this was very hard for him. He was an amazing ER doctor and a very caring and compassionate human being. I pray he never loses his love for his patients. As we departed and started toward the waiting room, I didn't know how to tell our family that Elly had gone home. Steve and I could not think of the right words, for our minds had been shattered and our hearts had been broken. As we walked into the waiting room, everyone knew that it was over, except for her sisters. Steve and I said, in broken and empty voices, "It's time to go home." Lindsey and Jesi looked up and asked, "Without Elly?" We burst into tears. This had been the most devastation this family had ever incurred. From this day forth, our lives changed forever. This day, May 21, 1998, our daughter, Elly Elizabeth, went home to heaven at 5:00 a.m. *The grieving begins.*

As we drove home that day, everything was still, and silence engulfed us. We were empty. There was no emotion or sound heard in the car. That day, a part of me died as well. I was now left to pick up the pieces, so I thought. The pieces that had been broken were about to be put together by Jesus, in a way I could not have imagined.

As one journey ends, another begins.

Another Journey Begins

Before I start talking about this part of the journey, I need so desperately for you to understand the reason for this book. The Lord laid upon my heart to write an article about our daughter a few months after she died. So, I did just that. In my mind, I thought this would help someone who has a child with this syndrome. I wrote the article and kept it. I never did anything with it. Why? I was not sure, until now. I believe it wasn't the correct time. I also believe it was a healing process for me. As I write this book today, twenty-some years later, I am in a place where it is time for this story to be told. Elly remains in our hearts! She remains with us in spirit! We will be reunited with her when it's time for US to go to heaven. But for now, we are here to do the will of God, for I see my assignment set before me.

This story is written with the heart beat of love, in hopes that it will reach multitudes of families, to let them know that they were never alone in the death of their child nor were they forsaken. You may feel that your prayers were not answered. I know I did in MY time of grief, for I was filled will all kinds of emotions. However, a very wise man said to me, "The only person you are hurting is yourself. It doesn't do you any good to be mad at God." My husband was so very right in that statement, and it changed my life forever. I didn't know what would lay before me, but I certainly wanted to understand more and more of God. I started to delve into the knowledge, understanding, wisdom, and revelation of the Word. However, I am getting ahead of myself. Let us back up!

I pray this story touches *all* hearts. I pray that it will inspire a young doctor to research this syndrome called *Pearson syndrome* and strive for a cure. Until this day, I will pray! I pray for all children, sick and healthy alike. As I have seen in my life, children are an inspiration. They so undeniably offer love and compassion, they give joy and laughter, and they show us true strength.

At the end of Elly's road, God was reaching out to her with open arms. I know now that is where all my answers will be waiting for me. Until then, all of us who are faced with a tragedy in our lives need to keep in mind that we are never alone. There is always someone out there who has gone through a similar trial. We all have our crosses to carry. Think about what Jesus did for us when he carried that magnificent and deadly cross. He showed us what unconditional love is and the meaning of life. It is the little things that matter most and the little things that are brought in by love. Until you are faced with all of life's challenges, you cannot even begin to understand the reasons why people do what they do, the decisions they make, or how they are feeling, etc. We should never judge one another but love one another. Always look at the big picture in front of you. Try to put yourself in that person's shoes or maybe you have walked in that person's shoes. Then and only then, you can get a glimmer of understanding with your heart, and then love that person without judgment. Always keep your eyes on Jesus, and you will walk the love walk. How do we do this? Keep on reading the *Heart Beat of Love*, and see what love Jesus gives us all.

Would you give up your life to save your child? I believe you would in a heart beat. Why? Because of love. Why did Jesus give up His life to save you? *Again* because of love. Can you see this love? Can you understand this love? Can you even begin to comprehend this love? Can you make sense of this love?

I cried tears of sorrow then, because of death. I cry tears of joy now, because of life! After Elly's death, I began to experience some supernatural events. These events drew me into such a strong yearning to know more about the Son of God. I began an investigation into this phenomenon called Jesus Christ. This path led me directly to my Savior, with a supernatural understanding of who He is, both Son of Man *and* Son of God! "He is the one who is, who was, and who is to come" (Revelation 1:4–7 NIV). *He* was the one who sent the Holy Spirit to guide me and help me on this journey! When we are able to look beyond our human capacities and see the creation God has made, then we are able to begin to see through the eyes of Jesus.

The Light

I must say, I have experienced the ultimate light from God three times in my walk after Elly. Remember though, I also experienced this supernatural light the day Elly died. So in total, I experienced this light four times. Each time this light was encountered was completely unexplainable, beautiful, warm, and full of love. This light was a supernatural happening, if you will, a happening from Jesus.

Prior to Elly's funeral, if I recall correctly, it was the day we had arrived home from the hospital. The funeral director came to see Steve and myself in regard to the preparations of the funeral. The questions he was asking were difficult to answer. We truly never gave it a thought as to where we would like her buried, what type of casket, what clothes we would like her buried in, or if we wanted to have a viewing. He also asked what scriptures we would like read at her mass. I was hearing him, but I couldn't in my mind comprehend nor give answers. How could I even be burying my daughter? How does that even happen? The funeral director reviewed information with us as to how this process works. I was very grateful and thankful for his kindness. He was exceptionally kind and compassionate as he guided us through the steps. He completely understood our loss and that was truly apparent.

The day of our daughter's funeral, Steve, Lindsey, Jesi, and I woke up that morning and started preparations for the day. I remember feeling numb, as though my body was walking on this earth, but my spirit was not. I remember it being a beautiful sunny day. As we drove to the funeral home, I was blank. I knew I had helped our beautiful daughters get ready, and I remembered they were playing and laughing, but it was all blurred. You see, I was in shock. The shock left my body numb, it left my mind numb, and it left my heart numb. The funeral director was a gentle and loving man, full of grace and kindness. He was a rock for us that day.

I need to make this comment. As time went on through my love walk, I began having flashbacks of people, places, and things that took place from the time of Elly's death until the time of my new beginning. These flashbacks, as I have learned now, were experienced for a reason. The reason was to bring back what I could not fathom at the time of my grieving experience and bring it to the forefront of my mind, to the perfect place and time I could deal with it. The flashbacks were vivid pictures of moments, lost or stolen, that would come back to my memory in a second with the complete recollection of an experience. This always seemed to happen to me as I was driving my car somewhere. It was always when I was alone, but never thinking of anything in particular. The flashbacks would leave just as fast as they had come, giving me an "aha" moment, and then I would begin to cry. It was a healing process. It was also a learning process.

As decisions were made and clothes picked out, family and friends came to see us to express their sympathies. It was so greatly appreciated; however, I knew they were there, but please remember, I was not. We decided to have the funeral without the viewing. Of course, family met before the funeral for prayer. All our family members came with much support and love. All of Elly's nurses from the skilled and professional services, from her pediatrician's office, friends, and family came to say their last good-byes. The church was full of love. At times like this, people come together to offer their love and support. I wonder, why can't we always give this love daily? Aren't we supposed to? After the funeral service, we met everyone outside who attended the mass so they could offer their condolences. They just couldn't bring themselves to leave without giving us warm hugs and kisses. It was very emotional but very warm and sincere.

After the greetings, we arrived at my brother Don's house for a luncheon. As I stood back, I watched everyone talking, eating, laughing, sharing stories, etc. I stood there thinking, *Why are you laughing? My daughter is dead and you are laughing!* Thank goodness, I only thought this and didn't let it come out of my mouth. I remember saying to my husband, "Let's go! It's time to go! We need to go see

Elly." I was talking about going to the cemetery. He understood my urgent request, so we left together, leaving our daughters with family, and went to the cemetery. This was one of the moments that I experienced Jesus's loving light. We stood beside her grave, and I remember feeling an extraordinary light shining down on us with such awesome warmth. Oh, you could say it was the sunlight. Yes, you could say this; however, it was not! It was much more than the warm rays streaming down from the sun. This light was streaming down from the heavens. It was supernaturally bright with a piercing warm glow that enveloped us as it did when we were holding Elly as her spirit slipped out of her body and went home to heaven. It was a magnificent light! Yes, many tears were shed for quite some time. I will never forget this light. This light is key!

As time passed from the day of the funeral and when the sympathy cards no longer came in the mail, I would visit Elly every day at the cemetery. I would talk to her and pray. I know my husband did this as well. There was one particular day, as I was sitting by her grave, talking to her and Jesus, I felt a serenity that I never felt before. It was such an overwhelming peace that just consumed me. I knew at that moment it was okay to go home and begin to live again as a wife and mother in the complete sense of those statuses. As I was driving, this light appeared again! It was blinding, but yet I could see clearly as I was driving down the road. It was almost like I was being led, and yes, of course, I followed. I arrived home with such peace. I did not understand this light at that time. Did I share this light? Absolutely! Did people believe me? Hmm, I don't know. I can only guess that a few may have thought that I was just grieving and needed something to believe in, so they let it go. Ha, ha, ha! I can only imagine what they thought.

The day after this, stranger experiences began happening. Our alarm clock started going off at 5:00 a.m. every morning. This lasted for approximately three weeks. We did not have our alarm set for this time. It just kept waking us up. My husband and I discussed the fact that this was the exact time Elly died. This was a very meaningful time. Was this a way of communication? What was the reason? We didn't know.

On different occasions, my husband and our daughter Lindsey saw Elly. In the spirit, that is. Steve saw her standing on the bed in between us one night as I was sleeping. He said it was amazing! I believed him and yet thought, *Why am I not seeing her?* Lindsey saw her in church dressed in white with a magnificent light shining through her. She said that Elly was so beautiful and that somehow she was in the air by a stained-glass window. I remember seeing Lindsey looking at this window in church, but at that time, I had no idea what she had truly seen. Jesi and I never saw her as they did. I did pray for the ultimate gift of seeing her again. I so badly wanted to see her. So desperately wanted to see her!

It was a beautiful summer's day when Lindsey and Jesi had friends come over to play. I was doing laundry. Our laundry room was right next to our kitchen. I saw this little girl all in white walk by me. I leaned over into the kitchen and said, "Honey, is there anything you need? Would you like something to eat or drink?" When I leaned over and saw no little girl in the kitchen, I felt goosebumps start from the middle of my back and go all the way up into my neck! And as any adult would do, I bolted out the door and ran over to my mom's house. When I realized what I had done, I started to laugh. I thought, *What is wrong with you!* I explained to my mom what I had seen and experienced, and we laughed together. As fast as I ran there and explained this happening, I ran back home to check on our girls and their friends. They were having a wonderful time playing. They never even knew I left. My family and I experienced supernatural happenings or supernatural connections for quite some time thereafter. I believe these happenings were to get me and my family back on track in our daily lives.

One day Lindsey, Jesi, and I were heading out for a day of fun. As we were backing out of our driveway, we came up onto the road. Before I started to drive forward, within an instant, we all saw a beautiful, unexplainable white ball of light that came flashing down from the sky right before us but never hit the ground. As quickly as it came, it vanished! It reminded us of a falling star; however, it was much more than that. It was magnificent! What did we do? We were in such awe, we sat there and asked each other if we saw the same thing. And our responses were *yes*. We were all so excited, and yet we were all moved by this awesome wonder!

Approximately six months after Elly's death, I experienced another happening that took place during sleep, or was I awake? I really can't say. I remember it vividly. I was lying next to my husband, with my head and knees pointing toward him. My back was on the mattress, and my arms were spread out. I hope you can envision this. Suddenly I felt something or someone pulling my left arm. It was so intense that I could not move nor could I scream out for help. I tried so very hard to scream to my husband who was right beside me. All of a sudden, this incredible light came upon me! Yes, it was the same light that I had experienced before. It held me down with such power, warmth, and love. It held me there until the pulling on my left arm subsided. It seemed as though it was an eternity, but it was not. After this episode, I was baffled as to why this happened. I have my thoughts on this. I will leave it up to your imagination, or should I say I will leave it in your heart, and you will see how it unfolds. Was it God? Was it Satan? Was it the light guarding and protecting me from the darkness? Hmm.

Let's read on.

Now as time went on, my husband and our girls went on living their lives through work and school, and I found myself lost. I delved into books. I might add, I didn't read the correct book, the Bible. Give me time, I do get there! I needed to know what happens after death. I needed to understand the signs that we were experiencing and what they meant. I needed to know that there was life after death. But how? I read and read. I read spiritual books. I sought out at least a half a dozen psychics and mediums, looking for answers. I remember one day, in particular, going to see a medium. I became very anxious and sick to my stomach, for I had envisioned her as a woman of eccentricity. As I entered her house, I saw that it was normal. She wasn't dressed as a gypsy as I had expected. My anxiousness withered away. I did not want my future read at all, but I so badly wanted to hear from Elly. That was my ultimate goal. It was a nice reading, which confirmed a few things about the past. But the things that she confirmed really don't matter to me now because of my personal relationship with Jesus. Back then, I was just clinging onto whatever possible thing I could. As time went on, I saw other psychics, some that I was not impressed with and some that downright terrified me. I eventually distanced myself from this type of spirituality, as I understand it now to be deception. Our answers are not in psychics or mediums. Our answers are in God.

How do we find them? In the Bible. It clearly states this in John 1:1 (NIV), "In the beginning was the Word, and the Word was with God, and the Word was God." This, my friends, was the beginning of my obedient walk with God!

The Callings

I felt as though my family was moving forward in life without me and that I was left behind, trying to pick up the pieces of my role in this world. I was fearful that I would be lost. Well, I needed not to have worried. One morning, I woke up out of the blue and decided it was time for me to go back to work. This was eighteen months after Elly's death. I applied for a clerical job under an umbrella company covering multiple services, was accepted, and started back into the work field without a hitch. I was happy to do so, and I so enjoyed my fellow workers. They were an amazing group of people! I believe I was to start out here, to learn and experience the developmental and also the mental health aspect of children and adults. It was refreshing, and I enjoyed working at my job.

Just as quickly as I woke up one morning and decided to go back to work, the same experience happened to me two years later. I woke up one morning, went to work, and sat down with my supervisor. I stated that I was resigning and that I was going back to school for nursing. I sat there looking at my supervisor with such peace, and yet, at the same time, with a look of "What did I just do?" I could not believe those words had come out of my mouth! However, I had spoken it, and I knew deep within me that this was to be my next step in life. Now, mind you, I had been playing with the thought of going back to school but never said that I was going to do it. As a matter of fact, I kept talking myself out of it. I thought that I would not be good enough in math or chemistry. So, to be truthful, I had just been entertaining this idea. Imagine then how I felt when I blurted out, "I am going back to school." I must say, I had such a peace within me. I didn't have anything set up to go back to college. No details were worked out. I went home and told my husband what I had done, and he was so kind and gracious that he encouraged me and backed me up. All went smoothly, and I began my nursing courses that fall. Mind you, I resigned from my job in the summer and began school in the fall. God's plan? Yes, I believe so.

It took me three years to complete my associate nursing degree. Since I was an older student in her thirties, I needed to begin as a nontraditional student and had to take courses that I once had already taken but the credits would not transfer. No worries, I thought to myself, I can do this! As you can guess, I did graduate on time and started working right after graduation. I went through college without any issues. I had tutors, and I am not ashamed to admit that, and they were exceptional. I never stopped being a mother, but as a mother, I continued on as a wife, mother, and student. Did I have tests and trials along the way? I mean tests and trials not only with school, but life? Absolutely, but I never gave up. There was always something pushing me. Hmm…I wonder what it was? I know now, but I didn't then. Please keep reading this journey with me. There were nights I was too exhausted to study for a test or do work, but I kept on pushing through. When I look back at my experiences, I captured the gift that God so preciously bestowed upon me. It was his compassion and mercy. God pushed me on my path that He created for me.

I had many interviews; so therefore, I had my choice of positions. I chose the hospital that offered a job on the pediatric floor. I worked the night shift, for all new nurses start there. I didn't mind at first, for I knew I would work up. I was so excited for I thought, *Wow, this position was meant for me! Since I had lost my daughter, I could help other children.* I was so excited. I worked a few weeks and realized that this was not for me. I questioned myself, because all through college this is what I had wanted. Key, what I had wanted, but was it what God wanted? You see, even when we get off course, God is always there to put us back on track.

I saw a position for an RN in a nearby hospital. I applied and had a wonderful interview. I can remember it as clear as day. I was talking with the supervisor of this position, and she asked me, "What animal would you describe yourself as?" I looked at her as I repeated the question. I said, "I believe a koala bear." When I heard that come out of my mouth, I started to giggle. I thought to myself, *Tricia, what on earth, why would you say such a thing!* She asked why. Please remember there wasn't any time for preparation for this question, so out of my mouth came, "Because they are a kind and compassionate animal. I look at myself as kind and compassionate person, and I believe that is what all people need." Now I didn't know if koala bears were kind and compassionate. So why I had said that, God only knows. She looked at me and smiled. I thought to myself, *Well, Tricia, I believe that was not a good answer*, as I chuckled to myself. She told me that she had a position in the emergency room and asked if I would like it. I was shocked! I said, "Oh my I don't have any experience..." and before I could get another word out, she said, "Nurses don't have to have experience. You learn from experience, and I believe you would be a good fit." I accepted the position, and once again I wondered what I had done? I was terrified of the unknown! I thought, *Oh my God!* Well, as it turns out, I absolutely enjoyed being an ER nurse. I learned so much from the other nurses and doctors. We were like a family. Becoming a nurse doesn't mean you can't expand in your profession, and believe me, you most certainly can.

I have changed jobs through the years and have enjoyed all of them immensely. I have worked in wellness programs, outpatient psychiatric clinics, and schools. I even worked in a program that was a bridge between mental health and physical health. That was an amazing journey. I believe that God has chosen us for a reason, and as I learn, study, and meditate on the Word, I am growing in wisdom, knowledge, understanding, and revelation. Praise Jesus!

As you recall, I had written an article on Elly's journey six months after her death; however, I never published it. I never felt the leading to do so. However, I always had a desire to write a book on Elly's syndrome to maybe touch others with her journey. I never really knew where to begin...or end. So, this book was always in the back of my mind. I believe it was a healing process for me. However, I knew one day I would be writing a book. Well, here we are. Let me take you on this journey that leads us up to the present. I was working two part-time jobs when I had a desire to quit the one in order to continue writing this book. I needed that extra gentle push by God to do so. One day, just like the day I quit my other job to start college, I quit my job without hesitation and had such a peace and joy. It was time for me to finally begin again and finish writing this book. This is my journey now, compiling what I have written thus far and beginning the actual writing process. What would this book entail? God knows that answer. Along with my knowing that this book needed to be finished, God who is so good gave me a confirmation by a pastor's wife. I was thrilled! I still didn't know the hows or the wheres, but I did know that it was time.

You see, God made this book so apparent, for it is about love! And who is love? God. I am streamlining this book from Elly's heart beat of love to Jesus's heart beat of love. I have spoken of love of family and friends. Now I will speak on the love of Jesus! If you really look into your heart, you will find that every heart beat is of Jesus, isn't it?

Obedience

A while back when I was working long hours in the emergency room, I met up with another nurse who introduced me to my dear and close friend of approximately fourteen years. She is the one I hired to house clean, and she is the one who introduced me to the Bible. As I said before, I don't believe in coincidence, but I do believe we all have a calling from God—whether it is a job, a ministry, a hobby, or whatever you would like to call it, it is from God. He gets us back on track to what He wants us to do whether we go willingly or fighting. We may not even be certain we are going down the right path, but does this really matter? God is the creator of all creation. So think about it. He moved the stars, the planets, his apostles, and so much more as though we are a game of chess. However, he always places us where He needs us to be.

Do you understand? God created the heavens, Jesus led his disciples and asked them to expand to preach the gospel, Paul was led by the Holy Spirit to reach the world, and you will find more as you read the Bible. So never fear of walking down the wrong path; be reassured that He will get you on the correct one. So as mentioned, I met Vicki through a coworker and friend who introduced me to her. She agreed to help me out. Vicki began cleaning for me within a week or two. Let me tell you, she was an amazing help not only with house but with my understanding of the Bible! As time went on, Vicki and I started talking more about God, about the Bible, and about life. I became fascinated by all my life experiences, not only through Elly's journey but even through my own childhood encounters.

Next, Vicki invited me to her Bible study. I was thrilled! These women at this Bible study were so fascinating and knowledgeable. I truly learned what I needed to know and more. I am so very thankful for these ladies, and they are still in my life today. As time went on, my daughters Lindsey and Jesi also started to attend the Bible study. Let me tell you, not only did we begin to understand the Bible, but we became *strong* in the Lord! I am so very proud of Lindsey and Jesi. They truly are daughters of Jesus, and they are raising powerful babes, which are my grandbabies. I don't want to get ahead of myself, so let me start telling you about this journey of obedience.

It took some time to understand the books of the Bible. At first, I was so overwhelmed by it all, but yet, I was so excited! After Elly's death, I needed to know and understand more and more about life after death. I needed to learn of my Father in heaven, Jesus, and the Holy Spirit. Three in One! I had such a strong desire to keep moving forward in my faith walk as well as my *love* walk, and I was determined not to quit. Today, I am still learning more and more of the Word, which is Jesus. It is so fascinating to me! I finally understood how to navigate the Bible, and I was able to understand the Word. You may think that I'm a Bible scholar by now, right? *Too funny.* I had so much to learn, and I am still learning.

I went to church every Sunday with my family as a little girl, and now with my husband and family. I sat in the pew and listened as we followed along in the missalette. That is quite different from actually researching and knowing the Bible. Reading the Bible takes you to a deeper and more loving level. It takes you into the heart of God! I was not able to understand this on my own account, but I WAS through the Holy Spirit. You see, when I became born again, I accepted Jesus into my heart. He now lives inside of me today. This is called the indwelling of the Holy Spirit. I am saved through Jesus. I also asked for the infilling of the Holy Spirit to guide me. I asked Him to take up residency in my heart, to ensure that His *love* would continue to grow. My body is the temple of the Holy Spirit! What an exciting adventure! I knew thereafter that my soul and body would be renewed in the Word, and that I was now a woman of Christ.

As the Holy Spirit dwells in me and is upon me, I am able to take on this adventure of faith with certainty of *who i am in* Jesus and what my walk looks like in this life. I was not able to do this prior to the Holy Spirit, for the Word did not make sense to me. It was like reading a story that had no story line nor could I comprehend the words. They were getting so far away from my comprehension that I just gave up on it. I was so caught up on the lineage that bored me, and the language of the KJV (King James Version) blew me away. So, I put the Bible down. Now, I can say the Words are alive! Jesus is alive! They transport me back to the time of the Old Testament and the New Testament. From the beginning to the end, from Genesis to Revelation. There is so much wisdom, knowledge, understanding, and revelation that comes from this book. I have focused more of my attention on the New Testament, especially the Epistles. These books tell us who we are in Christ and share with us how we are to live. The gospels show us the path Jesus walked, and we are to walk as He. We are to listen and understand Jesus as He walks us through this book with our eyes wide open ready to *see*, our ears wide open ready to *hear*, and our hearts wide open ready to *receive the blessings* He has given us, and our voices wide open to *share Jesus*. It is an amazing read!

Please know, it is much easier to understand the Bible with the teaching of the Holy Spirit versus you trying to read through this by yourself. Also, I suggest to always start out with a study Bible, which will give you a deeper explanation of the scripture verses. There are a few Bibles out there; you just need to find one that speaks to you in a fashion you are able to understand. Don't let your ignorance or maybe laziness lead you astray. Trust me, reading this book bestows upon you so many promises of God. It shows us that God is love and love is God. It shows us the love commandment that we walk today. It gives us clarity of who we are in Christ. It speaks to our hearts to renew our minds. It is so much wrapped up in one book. What I have mentioned is just a tiny fragment of what is in this amazing book. You can call this the book of love, of prophecy, of blessings, of promises, and so much more! Today, make a promise to yourself to become acquainted with the Bible. Take some time out of your busy day, and sit down with this amazing book, and let it teach you!

Words of advice:

1. Ask Jesus to read this to you.
2. Ask Him for wisdom to understand His Word.

3. Ask Him to come into your heart to better comprehend Him.
4. Ask Him to lead you into the path He has for you.

Trust me, you will not be disappointed! I have been reading the Bible for quite sometime now on a daily basis. Each reading session, I am learning and understanding something new each time. It is amazing! I take what the Bible states and get into a conversation with the Holy Spirit for better understanding. How do I do this? I pray before my Bible time, and I ask for guidance. I ask for deeper wisdom, knowledge, understanding, and revelation. I then offer thanksgiving, praise, and worship to the Father, Son, and Holy Spirit. After my readings, I meditate on a verse that jumps out at me. Remember the Word is alive, and it will transport you to a life of meaning within minutes. What an amazing and blessed way to start your day! Does it always have to be in the morning? No, but it sure starts your day with a blessing! John 1:1 (NIV) says, "In the beginning was the Word, and the Word was with God, and the Word was God." John 1:14 (AMP) says, "And the Word [Christ] became flesh, and lived among us; and we [actually] saw His glory, glory as belongs to the [One and] only begotten Son of the Father, [the Son who is truly unique, the only One of His kind, who is] full of grace and truth [absolutely free of deception]."

As I have mentioned, the Bible is an excellent read, *but* it is so much more than that. What you read, you must do. Act upon the Word. Soak it in. Meditate on it. Speak it. *Live it!* There is a difference between reading a book and living it. Right? The Word is Jesus, *who* is alive. The Word is alive! Do you see? You may also want to join a Bible study group. Just a suggestion. I have read many books from credible authors, and I have also watched many videos. Word of caution. Although I was helped tremendously through these authors and have watched some videos, please be aware and always test what you read. Meaning, go to the Bible to see if that is what the scriptures are truly saying. If it is not in the Bible, then most definitely it is false. Be aware! I am not saying this to frighten you in any way. I simply want to make you aware of the fact that there are teachers out there who are not entirely truthful. Whether they have been taught that way or their intent is to lead you away from Jesus, either way, go to the Bible and let it speak to you. The Bible is the only book you need; however, it is nice to get someone else's outlook and perspective. Just make sure you don't get into a habit and take their word for it. Don't get lazy and listen to others. Instead listen to Jesus and take His Word for it!

Now let's talk about obedience. Obedience means being reverent to God. The Word talks about obedience.

> And this is love; that we walk in obedience to His commands. (2 John 1:6 NIV)

> Because of the service by which you have proved yourselves, others will praise God for the obedience that accompanies your confession of the gospel of Christ, and for your generosity in sharing with them and with everyone else. (2 Corinthians 9:13 NIV)

> We are destroying sophisticated arguments and every exalted and proud thing that sets itself up against the [true] knowledge of God, and we are taking every thought and purpose captive to the obedience of Christ, being ready to punish every act of disobedience, when your own obedience [as a church] is complete. (2 Corinthians 10:5–6 AMP)

Please know that there are many scriptures concerning obedience throughout the Bible. I just wanted to share a glimpse into these scriptures that bring about a new understanding and a new journey into obeying God.

My journey started back in the beginning of our Bible studies when the Lord would come to me in a vision. He would show me words and pictures. One night, I went down into our basement and sat down on the couch to pray. As I prayed, I felt this urge to pick up a pen and paper and begin to write. So of course, I went upstairs, found a notebook and pen, and went back down to the couch. I was filled with such an overwhelming sense of *joy*. It surrounded me. That night, I began to write. I am still writing today, messages that Jesus shares with me. One way Jesus brings my attention to writing is by showing me a vision of a book with a feathered pen. I didn't realize what this meant at first, but now I am getting quite used to Him nudging me to write. This is our special time together. Thus far, the Lord and I have written approximately forty-seven messages. Now they most certainly did not start off detailed but very simple. Now when I see that symbol of the book and feathered pen, I know it is time to sit down and let the Holy Spirit flow.

Obedience is obeying the Word of God and acting upon the scriptures. It is amazing to read the Bible in order to understand God. *But* it is more incredible when you start obeying God, going out into this world doing what you have been instructed to do by the Holy Spirit! You see, we are not to fear, "For God hath not given us a spirit of fear, but of power, and of love, and of a sound mind" (2 Timothy 1:7 KJV). It also states in 1 Timothy 6:12 (NIV), "Fight the good fight of faith." Meaning, fight your fear with the Word. Don't let fear inhibit your walk with Jesus. Let Jesus walk with you. Your obedience will be the walkway into supernatural living.

We spoke about obedience; however, to really gather the concept of this, we need to delve into the love walk in further detail. You see, in order to be obedient, you need to understand God's love. I have a few messages that the Lord has shared with me, and I'd like to share them with you. Let's see what God's love is truly like!

Back in January of 2019, the Lord came to me. He discussed greater knowledge on the understanding of His love. Let me share this with you. Keep in mind, the scriptures you are about to read in regard to God's supernatural love are just a few samples of what is in the Bible. The Bible is a love story. It is an adventure. It is our reality! Please remain patient with me awhile longer, and we will see where the Holy Spirit leads us.

The New Year of Love (2019)

As you can see, He began leading me to scriptures that would best benefit my knowledge at that time. I truly believe since writing this book that His message of love coincides with my Elly's story. You ask, how? Please keep on reading.

When we look at Exodus 23:25–26 (NIV), it states, "Worship the Lord your God, and his blessing will be on your food and water. I will take away sickness from among you. And none will miscarry or be barren in your land. I will give you a full life span." **I truly believe God's will is for our healing, health, and wholeness. I believe and trust in the Word. So as it states, love produces healing and retains God's promises. I believe you may be asking yourself at this point, "What is she talking about? Didn't her daughter die even though she prayed for healing?" Yes, I did pray, but even though Elly died, that was not the end. I became stronger in my faith and in God's love. As I continued to seek Jesus, I realized something about myself. I could not punish myself for thinking I didn't have enough faith. Nor could I punish myself for not praising Him enough or not standing on His Word. Heck at that time, I was still walking by my religious faith and not by my personal relationship with God. At that time, I didn't know the difference. But with that said, at that time, I truly believed in my God and His almighty power. I still believe in Him today. I believe with my whole heart and soul that God *saved* my daughter! He did not give this syndrome to her. Let me repeat: He did not give this syn-**

drome to her! I don't have all the answers as to why some children and adults die and some do not, but what I do know is that I will keep on praising Him in the storm, and I will praise Him in the Joy. I will praise Him forever.

How grand a statement. When we really have a personal relationship with Jesus, our Lord and Savior, we then can begin to determine the will of God. The Word is truth, and the Word is His will. Keep this in mind as we go forth with this message.

Psalm 100:5 (AMP) states, "For the Lord is good; His mercy and lovingkindness are everlasting, His faithfulness [endures] to all generations." **God's love is never-ending. It is unfailing, and it is fulfilling. He never leaves us nor does He abandon us in our time of need. As you can see in the details thus far, it shows God with us. As a matter of fact, it shows the healings and miracles that took place throughout Elly's journey. We still see them today. Oh my, yes, they may not be what we expect or think they should be, but if we just take a moment to see the beauty around us and smell the sweet aroma of God, we will then begin to see God's promises and blessings.**

So just imagine. God's love is unfailing! Is your love unfailing? Do we allow our thoughts, emotions, and mentality to interfere with our decision making about someone or something? Do we let that sway us, one way or another, when it comes to loving someone? You see, God is not a feeling or emotion. He is our creator. He is a God who loves His children unconditionally. Yes, that's right. Unconditionally! It doesn't matter if you are a Christian or a nonbeliever. *He loves us the same.* What a powerful statement! God, Jesus, and the Holy Spirit love us no matter what. Yes, and Amen! *Wow.* Isn't He an amazing God? Absolutely! So since God loves us and He is our Father in heaven, He will let us go through tests and trials. But never more than what we can handle. You see since God created us, He Knows us. Therefore, He knows how much we can tolerate. It states in Jeremiah 1:5 (NIV), "Before I formed you in the womb I knew you, before you were born I set apart you." The only stipulation, if you would call it that, is this: He also gave us free will; so therefore, we have the choice to make him Our Lord and Savior. We have the choice to invite Him into our hearts. Are you ready to do so? Let's keep reading.

Psalm 103:3–5 (NIV) states,

> Who forgives all your sins and heals all your diseases. Who redeems your life from the pit and crowns you with love and compassion. Who satisfies your desires with good things so that your youth is renewed like the eagle.

Love renews and heals, and He covers us with His wings. God's will is healing! His will is written in the Word. And please do not forget that the Word is Jesus! He covers us in the shadow of His wings, and He guides, supports, and protects us (Psalm 91). However, we also must be obedient to His ever so soft voice as well as His bold voice. We must do our part in this love walk. And what is our part? To believe and trust in Jesus. To have personal confidence and trust in Him who gave us all. To keep the *faith*.

Can God's love really protect us and heal us? Why, of course it can. He gave His one and only Son. He gave us Jesus! Imagine God giving us His Son Jesus to save and free us all from darkness. I would say that is an unconditional love that no one can imagine. Or can you?

Jeremiah 31:3 (NIV) states, "The Lord appeared to us in the past, saying: 'I have loved you with an everlasting love; I have drawn you with unfailing kindness.'" **This scripture shows us that love never fails nor does it ever end**. As it states in Malachi 3:6 (NIV), "I the Lord do not change." In Hebrews 13:8 (NIV), it says, "Jesus Christ is the same yesterday and today and forever." His *love* never changes, for God never changes. His *will* never changes, for God never changes. Are you getting this?

God's love is infinite!

Matthew 5:43–48 (NIV) states,

> You have heard that it was said, "Love your neighbor and hate your enemy." But I tell you, love your enemies and pray for those who persecute you, that you may be children of your Father in heaven. He causes His sun to rise on the evil and the good, and sends rain on the righteous and the unrighteous. If you love those who love you, what reward will you get? Are not even the tax collectors doing that? And if you greet only your own people, what are you doing more than others? Do not even pagans do that? Be perfect, therefore, as your heavenly Father is perfect.

This is our pathway to walk in our love walk; these are the footprints we are to follow. Jesus never said this would be easy. Under the New Testament, we are to love. That is our commandment in the law of faith, to love! We are not to love with our flesh. You will understand this statement as we move forward. Come on, let us keep learning this message.

Mark 11:23, 24, 25 (NIV) states,

> Truly I tell you, if anyone says to this mountain, "Go, throw yourself into the sea," and does **not doubt** in their heart **but believes** that what they say will happen, it will be done for them. Therefore I tell you, whatever you ask for in prayer, believe that you have received it, and it will be yours. And when you stand praying, if you hold anything against anyone, **forgive them**, so that your Father in heaven may forgive your sins.

Love is forgiveness, and when you forgive and forget, your prayers will be answered. Don't harbor ill feelings; give them to

Jesus, and let Him take care of them for you. As it states in 1 Peter 5:7 (AMP), "Casting all your cares [all of your anxieties, all your worries, all your concerns, once and for all] on Him, for He cares for you [with deepest affection, and watches over you very carefully]." I myself like to take scripture and make it into a prayer. This helps me to meditate on it, and it renews my mind. For a prayer example from 1 Peter 5:7, "Thank you so gracious, merciful, and loving Father for taking my cares (my anxieties, my worries, my fears, and my concerns) once and for all. I refuse to ponder on them any longer, for I trust and stand on my faith in You. When a care comes to my mind, I shut it down, for I know you have it and took care of it. I refuse you anxiety, worry, fear, and concerns in Jesus's Name." This is where I have peace, shalom.

Forgiveness isn't easy. In order to forgive, you have to forget. What does this mean? I have heard many people say, "I forgive this person, but I will never forget what they have said or done." This truly isn't forgiving, is it? Truly forgiving is what Jesus gave to us upon His cross, where He hung taking away all our sins, sickness, and death. He gave us *life*, my friends. So if Jesus can forgive us, and believe me He does, why can't we forgive others? The answer to that is this: We live by our flesh, which is our thoughts, our feelings, our own will and emotions. So we live by our body and soul. We need to live by our spirit. You see, God is spirit, and Jesus is spirit, and he gave to us His Holy Spirit. So therefore, if you ask Jesus to reside in your heart, He will hook up with your spirit man, and you will be able to flourish in a way you have never seen before.

Listen, my friends. This is how I see it. The only one you are hurting (yes, let me say this again), the only one you are hurting is yourself. When you don't forgive, you lose the joy and peace that Jesus gave you. You lose the healing process. Why? Because you harden your heart. Take a little advice today, forgive that someone and move on. God actually forgets our sins. That is stated in Isaiah 43:25 (NIV), "I, even I, am he who blots out your transgressions, for my own sake, and remembers your sins no more." And again in Hebrew 10:17 (NIV), "Then He adds, 'Their sins and lawless acts

I will remember no more.'" This speaks volumes! Doesn't it? If God can forget and dismiss, then why can't we?

Mark 12:30 (NIV) states, "Love the Lord your God with all your heart and with all your soul and with all your mind and with all your strength." **This is your recipe for love. Just like any recipe, you need to have the correct ingredients, correct? So, the recipe you need for love is the Word, and yes, forgiveness. You need to understand God's grace and His mercy, which He bestows upon us as we should bestow upon others, shouldn't we? Yes, we should. Let us walk in the love of God**. Let go of the feelings you're harboring and give them to Jesus. You have freedom in Him. Take it! Luke 23:34 (NIV) states, "Jesus said, Father, forgive them, for they do not know what they do." **Look at His love. Is this not unconditional love, asking His Father to forgive them? Oh my, absolutely!**

Can you even imagine being able to ask your Father in heaven in Jesus's name to forgive the person who is persecuting you? What a happy day that will be when you reach that revelation and understanding. Do you know who else did this? Stephen in the book of Acts. It is mentioned below, and what an amazing story it is. As a matter of fact, it is incredible! Keep reading.

John 8:12 (NIV) states, "When Jesus spoke again to the people, He said, 'I am the light of the world. Whoever follows me will never walk in darkness but will have the light of life.'" **Jesus is love, so if He is the light, then the light is love. Let's substitute light with love in the following scripture.** When Jesus spoke again to the people, He said, "I am the love of the world. Whoever follows me will never walk in darkness but will have the love of life." He has already given us eternal life, if we have accepted Him into our lives. What an awesome grandeur to know that kind of love. Oh, by the way, you can have that kind of love. How? Keep reading.

Here it is! Acts 7:59–60 (NIV) states, "While they were stoning him, Stephen prayed, 'Lord Jesus, receive my spirit.' Then he fell on his knees and cried out, 'Lord, do not hold this sin against them.' When he said this, he fell asleep." Asleep means he died. **Look at the love Stephen showed in this passage. He followed in the footsteps of his Master, Jesus. He was an exceptional man, a *selfless* man**.

Can you imagine! A man of God showing so much mercy and grace upon the people who were persecuting him for his belief in Jesus. Jesus did the same thing as he hung on the cross for us and made the same statement, asking God to forgive those who persecuted Him. This is just the beginning of the love walk. As a matter of fact, Stephen was a stepping stone to Paul's salvation. At that time, however, Paul had no idea. Paul was the leader who persecuted the church and approved the stoning of Stephen. This is a heart-changing story. Please read this story when you have a moment. You will find such love; you will find God's love! For now, I must keep on our path.

Romans 8:14–17 (NIV) states,

> For those who are led by the Spirit of God are the children of God. The Spirit you received does not make you slaves, so that you live in fear again; rather, the Spirit you received brought about your adoption to sonship. And by him we cry "Abba, Father." The Spirit Himself testifies with our spirit that we are God's children. Now if we are children, then we are heirs—heirs of God and co-heirs with Christ, if indeed we share in his sufferings in order that we may also share in His glory.

God is love, Christ is love, the Holy Spirit is love, and we are love too! The key here is to know who you truly are in Christ Jesus. To know the truth of God. Did you notice that the Spirit Himself testifies with our spirit? You see, this is the truth because the Word which is God and which is in the Bible speaks truth. God does not lie.

Romans 12:9–10 (NIV) states, "Love must be sincere. Hate what is evil; cling to what is good. Be devoted to one another in love. Honor one another above yourselves." (To read more on Love in Action review verses 11 to 21.) You probably didn't think that while reading this book you would have homework, did you? It isn't so much homework as it is a fire to spark your spirit to begin your new adventure. This scripture states to be humble toward others. To be humble is to love one another. You are not looking from self-motives, but you are looking to Jesus. You see, we get so caught up in ourselves that we can't seem to get beyond us. That, my friend, is self-absorption. (selfish). We are not to be selfish but *selfless*. When we are selfless and cling to what is good, we then can start to serve others as Jesus has done for us. What an incredible way to walk by serving others in love!

In 1 Corinthians 2:14 (NIV), it states, "The person without the Spirit does not accept the things that come from the Spirit of God but considers them foolishness, and cannot understand them because they are discerned only through the Spirit." **To have love is to have the Spirit. The Spirit is love. He helps us in our love walk by leading us down the correct and narrow path toward Jesus. Yes, this path is narrow, but oh so rewarding. All we have to do is be obedient and follow the Holy Spirit. Yes, follow Him. Sometimes this is hard for us to do. Why? Because in order for us to be obedient, we may have to put down our phones, iPads, laptops, jobs, hobbies, etc. and follow Jesus. However, when we do all these things and stop looking to them as our gods, we will then follow our one and only God, our true God. We begin to make a difference, not only in our lives but in the lives of everyone around us.**

There you go, obedience. Shall we say that when we are obedient to God's Word (Jesus), then we are walking in God's love. When we walk in God's love, we are selfless and we are standing in God's joy and peace. Wow, we all can have this!

In 1 Corinthians 13:4–8 (AMP), it is God's recipe.

> Love endures long and is patient and kind; love never is envious nor boils over with jealousy; is not boastful or vainglorious, does not display itself haughtily. It is not conceited [arrogant] and inflated with pride; it is not rude [unmannerly] and does not act unbecomingly. Love [God's love in us] does not insist on its own rights or its own way, for it is not self-seeking; it is not

> touchy or fretful or resentful; it takes no account of the evil done to it [pays not attention to a suffered wrong]. It does not rejoice at injustice and unrighteousness, but rejoices when right and truth prevail. Love bears up under anything and everything that comes, is ever ready to believe the best of every person, it's hopes are fadeless under all circumstances and it endures everything [without weakening]. Love never fails [never fades out or becomes obsolete or comes to an end]. As for prophesy [the gift of interpreting the divine will and purpose], it will be fulfilled and pass away; as for tongues, they will be destroyed and cease; as for the knowledge, it will pass away [it will lose its value and be superseded by truth].

Love never fails, for god is love and love is God. **So therefore, God never fails! This is the complete definition in the Amplified Bible.**

I suggest, and this is only a suggestion, to personalize this scripture into prayer and thank the Almighty God for His love. Your words have power whether they are of life or death. So, let us speak life (positive) words and avoid evil (negative) words. Here is an example of what I mean when I say to personalize this scripture.

> Thank you, Father, that your love is in me, which endures long, for I am patient and kind. I am not envious, nor do I boil over with jealousy. I do not display love arrogantly. I am not conceited, arrogant, nor am I inflated with pride. I am not rude or unmannerly, and I do not act unbecomingly. Love (God's love) is in me, and I do not insist on my own way, for I am not self-seeking nor am I touchy or fretful or resentful. I do not take account of evil done to me nor do I pay attention to a suffered wrong. I do not rejoice at injustice

> and unrighteousness, but I do rejoice when right and truth prevail. Love is in me, which bears up under anything and everything that comes. I believe the best of every person. Love's hopes are fadeless under all circumstances, and I endure everything without weakening because of love. Love never fails. And I never fail in love, in Jesus's Name. Amen.

You see, as I write this message to you, I am working on becoming more and more like Jesus. Am I there? NO. Am I striving for this? Yes. Just like Paul states in Philippians 3:12 (AMP), "Not that I have already obtained it [this goal of being Christlike] or have already been made perfect, but I actively press on so that I may take hold of that [perfection] for which Christ Jesus took hold of me *and* made me His own. Isn't this what we all are striving for?

In 1 Corinthians 16:13 (NIV), it states, "Be on your guard; stand firm in the faith; be courageous; be strong. **Do everything in love." (This is key.)** When we do everything in love, we can reach our goals. But when we veer off our path, then we begin to walk in darkness. Sometimes we don't even realize it, but eventually, if you don't, someone will, and it will be addressed. The secret ingredient is to confess, repent, and move forward when you veer off your path. Do not dwell on the evil but cling to the good.

In 1 Corinthians 11:28–31 and 33 (NIV), it states,

> Everyone ought to examine themselves before they eat of the bread and drink from the cup. For those who eat and drink without discerning the body of Christ eat and drink judgment on themselves. That is why many among you are weak and sick, and a number of you have fallen asleep. But if we were more discerning with regard to ourselves, we would not come under such judgment. So then, my brothers and sisters, when you gather to eat, you should all eat together.

Churches should not be marked by their ego, personality, or power plays. Instead, a heart of love, humility, and service, combined with a sound understanding of doctrine, keeps preferences and opinions from turning into convictions. (Taken from the study Bible of Dr. David Jeremiah, NIV.) In other words, let's not judge one another. Let's love one another. We truly don't know what the other person has gone through or is going through, only God does. We are to ask God what we may help the person with, whether in prayer, kindness, and most importantly in love. Also, we need to forgive before partaking in the bread and blood of Christ. If we do not examine our soul, we may be hindering our prayers, our healing, and our intentions.

Galatians 2:20 (NIV) states, "I have been crucified with Christ and I no longer live, but **Christ lives in me**. The life I now live in the body, I live by faith in the Son of God, who loved me and gave himself for me." **Remember *this*: God is love, Christ is love, and we are love, for we have the Holy Spirit indwelling and infilling us**. This scripture is a strong verse if only you believe.

God so loved us that He gave us His one and only Son. Jesus gave us His *all*. So, to be able to say that we have been crucified with Christ is an honor. How do we gain this honor? Ask Jesus into your life now. Be true to yourself, and examine yourself. Are you really doing well without Him? Only you can answer that question. As for me, I do exceptionally well *with* Him. Without Him, I am nothing.

Galatians 5:6 (NIV) states, "For in Christ Jesus neither circumcision nor uncircumcision has any value. The only thing that counts is faith expressing itself through love." **Faith works by love; it doesn't matter whether we are a Jew or a gentile, we are all children of God. Remember, God is the creator, and He created us in His image (Genesis 1:27).** God is not a respecter of persons. What does this mean? He doesn't care who we are (our religion, culture, race, etc.). All He cares about is US. After all, He created us for a purpose. But remember, He also gave us freewill and choice. What are you doing with your freewill and choice?

Ephesians 3:6 (NIV) states, "This mystery is that through the gospel the Gentiles are heirs together with Israel, members together of one body, and sharers together in the promise of Christ Jesus." **We are all one; we are all the same in the body of Christ. We are equally loved.** This explains fully that God is not a respecter of persons.

Ephesians 5:19 (NIV) states, "Speaking to one another with psalms, hymns, and songs from the Spirit. Sing and make music from your hearts to the Lord." **This shows us how to love and interact with one another and with Jesus**. It also gives us a recipe in worship. Worship is giving praise and thanksgiving to our Father in heaven, Jesus Christ our Lord and Savior, and to the Holy Spirit. Did you know that the Holy Spirit is our comforter and counselor, our helper and advocate, our strengthener and intercessor, and our standby? God loves it when we worship Him! Did you know that we will be doing this in heaven? Yes, my friends, we will be worshiping and praising and thanking Him in heaven. We might as well get started here on earth, shall we?

Romans 8:28 (NIV) states, "And we know that in all things God works for the good of those who love him, who have been called according to his purpose." **To love God is to love one another.** To love God is to show him we are willing to do his purpose. We all have a purpose in life, don't we? Yes, we do! Isn't it time we start living for the purpose God so grandly created us for? Oh, you don't know your purpose? Keep your eyes on Jesus, be obedient, and follow Him. That is your purpose; then, all else falls into place.

Philippians 1:9–11 (NIV) states,

> **And this is my prayer: that your love may abound more and more in knowledge and depth of my insight, so that you may be able to discern what is best and may be pure and blameless for the day of Christ, filled with the fruit of righteousness that comes through Jesus Christ—to the glory and praise of God.**

When love abounds in our heart, we go into a deeper knowledge and insight with our Father in heaven, and we are able to discern without doubt. Love states it all, doesn't it? Love is Life!

Philippians 4:5 (NIV) states, "Let your gentleness be evident to all. **The Lord is near." Love is gentleness.** So if love is gentleness, then so are we. Are you starting to get the picture of what true love is? You see, even though we walk in gentleness, we also walk with boldness, meaning we walk with the confidence that Christ is in us!

Colossians 2:6–12 (NIV) states,

> So then, just as you received Christ Jesus as Lord, continue to live your lives in him rooted and built up in him, strengthened in the faith as you were taught, and overflowing with thankfulness. See to it that no one takes you captive through hollow and deceptive philosophy, which depends on human tradition and the elemental spiritual forces of this world rather than on Christ. For in Christ all the fullness of the Deity lives in bodily form, and in Christ you have been brought to fullness. He is the head over every power and authority. In him you were also circumcised with a circumcision not performed by human hands. Our whole self ruled by the flesh was put off when you were circumcised by Christ, having been buried with him in baptism, in which you were also raised with him through your faith in the working of God, who raised him from the dead.

Remember faith works by love only, and God is love. This is our makeup (form), for He is our creator.

Stand in faith by reading the Word. It states that faith cometh by hearing, and hearing by the Word of God (Romans 10:17, KJV). In other words, when you read the books of the Bible out loud, you become aware of the scriptures in an intimate way. It helps your mind align with your heart. Meaning? Spirit, soul, and body. Spirit is always first, then the soul and body line up with the spirit. This is the key. The Holy Spirit is the liaison between Jesus and you. Your spirit man renews your mind.

Colossians 3:17 (NIV) states, "And whatever you do, whether in word or deed, do it all in the name of the Lord Jesus, giving thanks to God the Father through Him." **Do it all in love**. Praise, worship, and giving thanks hourly for your blessings. If you don't see your blessings, just give honor to your Father in heaven, and your eyes will be opened.

James 2:13 (NIV) states, **"Mercy triumphs over judgment." This demonstrates the God kind of love.** Are you ready to show mercy toward others instead of judging them? Are you ready to accept God's mercy? As it states, Mercy triumphs over judgment! Today try to extend your hand of mercy toward others. I bet you will experience much joy when you show this act of kindness.

In 1 Peter 2:24 (NIV), it states, "'He himself bore our sins' in his body on the cross, so that we might die to sins and live for righteousness; 'by his wounds you have been healed.'" **This shows us that love produces healing**. What a powerful *impact*, by Jesus's stripes, we are healed! Jesus is love. When He was on the cross, He revealed His unconditional love by shedding His body and blood for us. When we take communion, remember the love our Lord and Savior demonstrated. The love He graciously gave to us. You may not realize this, but Jesus was beaten beyond recognition. He was broken, and then He became *whole*. He did all of this for us! Remember upon the cross when He said, "It is finished"? He finished it *all*. He defeated death and darkness for us, and He gave us His light, His *love*. When you put this into perspective, then how can you deny Him? You can't.

In 1 Peter 3:9 (NIV), it states, "Do not repay evil with evil or insult with insult. On the contrary, **repay evil with blessing, because to this you were called so that you may inherit a blessing."** We are heirs of God and coheirs with Christ; therefore, we are to follow in Christ's footsteps and show His love. Key, walk in Jesus's footsteps! We definitely show God's love when we can turn the other cheek and pray for one who does us wrong. Then, my friend, you know you are on the right path.

In 1 John 1:7 (NIV), it states, "But if we walk in light, as he is in the light, we have fellowship with one another, and the blood of Jesus, His Son, purifies us from all sin." **Light is love. The Spirit is love which stems from God's love. Once again, substitute light with love in the following scripture, and take note of the true meaning.** "But if we walk in love, as He is in love, we have fellowship with one another, and the blood of Jesus, His Son, purifies us from all sin."

In 1 John 3:14–15 (NIV), it states,

> **We know that we have passed from death to life, because we love each other. Anyone who does not love remains in death.** Anyone who hates a brother or sister is a murderer, and you know that no murderer has eternal life residing in him.

Love is life. Love is the tree of life, which is the tree of creation. Keep this scripture in your heart. Do you think it is ever too late to ask God for forgiveness? No. You may ask for forgiveness on your death bed and receive it. You may also ask Him into your heart and receive Him then. That is a wonderful time to acknowledge Jesus; however, my question to you is this: Why would you wait until then and miss out on all of His love and blessings? I encourage you today and every day to keep in mind what you have now and what you could have if you choose life with Jesus. We walk in a world of chaos. As we walk in this darkened world, Jesus's light penetrates through the darkness. If we stay in communion with Jesus, listen to Him, and walk with Him, no harm can come near us. Wow. Is it really that simple? Yes.

In 1 John 4:16–21 (NIV), it states,

> **And so we know and rely on the love God has for us. God is love. Whoever lives in love lives**

> **in God, and God in them. This is how love is made complete among us so that we will have confidence on the day of judgment: In this world we are like Jesus. There is no fear in love. But perfect love drives out fear, because fear has to do with punishment. The one who fears is not made perfect in love. We love because he first loved us. Whoever claims to love God yet hates a brother or sister is a liar. For whoever does not love their brother and sister, whom they have seen, cannot love God, whom they have not seen. And he has given us this command: Anyone who loves God must also love their brother and sister.**

This is a powerful scripture that brings this love picture altogether. I would say this scripture is the *glue.*

These scriptures we just reviewed are powerful; however, there are many scriptures in the Bible that discuss love. These are just a few that were brought to my attention by the Lord. These scriptures are a sequence that leads us into the depth of the understanding of God's love. Now let us talk about the *love* message that God gave me for this year, shall we? Come, take a walk with me. Let's explore a little deeper into this supernatural, unconditional love.

The Lord brought to my attention a shade chart of white, gray, and black a year ago. He said, "I had given this to you for a reason. Now is the time to use this demonstration." I was so happy to do so. As I gazed upon this chart, I understood that the white represents light or Jesus and that the black represents Darkness or Satan. However, I did not realize the depth until Jesus explained this to me. He asked me to delve into His deeper love, so I did, with the guidance of the Holy Spirit. Now, let's begin this new journey toward wisdom, knowledge, understanding, and revelation through the eyes of Jesus. Let's begin a complete *turn around,* if you will, a complete lifestyle change as we focus on His love. As you have read, love heals, forgives, brings riches and prosperity. It brings blessings upon those who truly believe, and it acts upon their faith. Jesus's love brings complete fullness of understanding, knowledge, wisdom, and revelation to the doers of the Word. As you fix your eyes upon Jesus and the distinction between the shade chart, you will realize one extraordinary factor. The denominator is *love*. God created all things in and through His love.

Please reference back to the above scriptures as needed. I am sure you will have questions, and I believe these scriptures will help answer your questions. As mentioned earlier, the Bible is a love story. Let's begin this new fashion of thinking and believing. Shall we?

White represents God, Jesus, and the Holy Spirit (the Holy Trinity). God is love and love is God. Just as the Word is God and God is the Word. White represents love, absolute unfailing love! White is *life*.

Black represents Satan, the king of darkness. He is the fallen angel Lucifer, who comes to kill, steal, and destroy. Darkness is empty; no love resides here.

Gray then represents us, the Christians. Now we need to understand the different shades of white, gray, and black to determine our walk in this chart. Let's refer to them as the lighter shade of gray and the darker shade of gray.

The lighter shade of gray, which is silver gray (this is the next shade up from gray) represents the Christians who are born again, believers, and are the temple of the Holy Spirit. They speak in tongues, meaning they pray in the Holy Spirit. They have a better understanding of the Word. But are they where they should be on their Holy walk? No, not yet. Are they willing to move forward to the whitest shade? Absolutely. Do they understand their true identity of love? Maybe so, but there is work that needs to be done on the inside of each Christian. **They need to exercise the God kind of love and follow the love commandment. They need to be doers of the Word and of the love!**

The darker shade of gray which is pewter gray (this is the next shade darker than gray) represents the Christians who are saved but yet they still live by the world, Satan's domain. Some are cemented in the religious system and some are sinking in quicksand. However, these Christians are still able to be drawn into the light. These Christians need our help! Do you see that God is calling us all Christians?

Now let's go to the next step. The next lighter color of gray, let's call this dove gray. These are Christians who understand the Word in its completeness. They are evangelists, apostles, prophets, teachers, and so forth. They truly understand love, but are they in the complete white? No. In order to get into the complete white of this chart, we need to walk and love like Jesus! Can we get there? Absolutely, by understanding what unconditional and supernatural love truly represents. It is the way of God's creation. It also is our choice! What choice will you make?

The next darker shade of gray we will call soft black. These are people who have completely lost their way in life. They have been enveloped by evil. Their souls are lost at this time. They refuse to repent and seek God. But do they still have a chance? Certainly. Remember, God is our creator; he is love. God trumps evil!

As you can see, the love walk, which is *your* walk with Jesus is a process, but it begins with love. It begins with understanding who we are in Christ and who we represent on earth, who is Jesus Christ. So to understand the steps, we have to understand the sequence to a glorious and eternal life.

We have different seasons in our love walk. We may have snow, rain, sun, wind, cold, and heat. We may have troubles, hardships, tests, and trials. We may have blessings, prosperity, healing, and health. One thing for sure is we need to stay in love, stay in God, and stay in the Word. As a matter of fact, do everything God's way!

Just imagine, God so loved the world that he gave us his one and only Son. Jesus so loved the world that he gave us His one and only life. He even descended into hell for us. Would you not say that this is a supernatural love, unconditional love, and a God kind of love? Are you willing to try to walk in this God kind of love? Is it even possible to have such an amazing love as God? Absolutely! How do I know this? It states it in the Word, and the Word does not lie because God does not lie! Are you getting excited yet? Just imagine that our heart can be so filled with love that it overflows to the next person and the next and the next. For this year and every year to come, my hope is that my heart will be overflowing with the God kind of love. I will not stop pressing forward in my walk with the Lord. Are you with me? Let us see where Jesus will take us. Take Jesus's hand and follow Him.

Remember, mercy triumphs over judgment. So let's not judge others, gossip, look down on, or surmise what someone is going through. Instead, let's approach one another with love, kindness, compassion, tenderheartedness, and respect. Let's approach one another with the God kind of love. You see, when we start acting like the world, we will hinder our healing and health processes. We will hinder our riches and prosperity. We will hinder our walk. Why? Because when we don't have love, we don't have God. And when we don't have God, we don't have faith. And when we don't have faith, we don't have belief. When we don't have belief, we don't have the light. Does this make sense to you? Do you see why walking in love, walking God's way, is so important? Do you see the majestic plan of our Father? God crowns us with love and compassion, so let's move forward in love and compassion. Let us not make excuses for ourselves any longer. When we are wrong, we are wrong. We need to repent quickly when we have wronged ourselves and others. Repent, hmm, what does that mean? This means to confess our sins to God and change our lifestyle into a God lifestyle. After this, then we can move forward. Our foundation is love. Our foundation is God. Our foundation is God who is love and who is our creator!

Did I say this would be easy? No. Will it be rewarding? Absolutely! This reward will be more than you could imagine or anything you could describe. Just read the scriptures and stand on them. Get them down into your spirit man, your heart brain if you will. Absorb them, eat them, drink them, meditate on them, and sleep on them. Let them fill you, and then you can say that you abide in the Word and the Word abides in you!

In closing, this love lesson showed us the difference between God's love and human love (1 Corinthians 13:4–8). Isn't the God kind of love the better avenue? Yes, hands down. Will it be easy? No. But when we stand strong in love, we will absolutely forgive, we will put others first, and we will walk hand in hand with God. We do not want to hinder our blessings, our healings and health, our spiritual riches and prosperity, nor do we want to hinder our relationship with God. Neither does God want us to turn away from Him. He has so many blessings He wants us to receive. He already embraced us with His love, so let's move forward and embrace others with His love as well. Let us share Jesus with others. Please remember, when we follow the Holy Spirit, He will guide us. With that said, even if we are not led to preach the gospel to individuals, we most certainly can show that we are Christians by our actions. As a matter of fact, Love is action, the Word is action, and God is action. As you know, repetition is good for your soul when it comes to reading the scriptures. This allows the scriptures to sink in, to be absorbed, and to enlighten your heart with knowledge, wisdom, revelation, and understanding.

Let us move forward this day and every day with the God kind of love and share His love with one another. **Let us be the love movement of God**! Are you ready? Are you ready to walk like Jesus?

Below you will see a picture the Lord encouraged me to draw. As you can see, I am not the artistic type; however, the message is quite clear.

In the Beginning…the "L" represents the Tree of Life (Tree of Creation). The "O" represents the crown of thorns that was placed on Jesus's head, which represents omnipresence, omnipotence, alpha, omega, the beginning and the end. He is the King of Kings and Lord of Lords. The "V" represents victory upon the cross with the crushing of His body and the dripping of His blood and water. This signifies the crushing of sin, darkness, and death. The "E" represents the Son Rise, the resurrection and eternal life in iridescent form (golden), **World Without End. Amen**.

Are you seeing the significance of God's love yet? Let's continue to get deeper into this love walk, shall we? The next message that God gave me speaks of His one and only Son. Keep in mind this is biblical.

Note: These messages have everything to do with our lives. As I look back, read, and remember our family's walk with Elly, I find more and more healings and miracles that took place each day of her beautiful life. When you keep Jesus as your main focus and not this world, your eyes are opened wide, and you see the Glory of God.

The One and Only Son

The Lord showed me a unique bond between Abraham and God Himself. They both gave up their one and only son, or did they? Hmm…you may be wondering at this time, Jesus was the one and only Son, but was Isaac? Keep in mind, Abraham also had a son who was his one and only by the spirit of God. Remember God anointed Abraham and Sara, and they conceived Isaac in their old age. God asked Abraham to sacrifice his one and only son to Him.

The test of Abraham (Genesis 22). Let me give you a brief summary of this story. As God asked Abraham to sacrifice Isaac to Him, Abraham obeyed by preparing a sacrificial altar. He stacked up sticks for the fire, tied up Isaac, and was ready to strike his one and only son with a knife. Right at that moment, the Lord called Abraham's name from heaven twice. Abraham said, "Here I am, Lord." What did the Lord tell him? "Do not lay a hand on the boy." Abraham's faith had conquered God's test. He was obedient and showed God his love by being willing to sacrifice his one and only son. So what did God do? He provided Abraham with a ram for the sacrifice (Genesis 22:1–19). So as you can see, Abraham had strong faith in his Lord. Isaac was set free, and many a blessing was bestowed upon Abraham's descendants. These blessings are as vast as the stars and as abundant as grains of sand on a beach. They multiply from generation to generation and from life to death. What does this mean? It magnifies God and blesses us! Since Abraham's seed has been blessed, it cannot be cursed. Once God gives blessings, He does not take them away. Are we not Abraham's seed? Yes, we are! Oh, but wait, this revelation becomes brighter than ever.

Now God sent his one and only Son, Jesus Christ, who became flesh and took up residency among us to glorify his Father with grace and truth (John 1:14 NIV). "For God so loved the world that He gave His one and only Son" to restore humanity back to its original state that was lost through Adam and Eve's sin (John 3:16 NIV). For whoever believes in His Son shall live and not die. For it states in 1 John 5:12 (AMP), "He who has the Son [by accepting Him as Lord and Savior] has the life [that is eternal]; he who does not have the Son of God [by personal faith] does not have the life." Since Abraham and his descendants were blessed with the inheritance, as vast as the stars, so was Jesus Christ of Nazareth. He also traveled the many particles of sand, and He has multiplied His seed from generation to generation, from descendants to descendants. HIS blessings will never be taken away, for He gave the ultimate gift of all. He was beaten and crucified beyond all recognition. He died for us, taking away all our sins, sickness, diseases, and pain. He went into hell to nullify death and was resurrected to give life to us. He gave us *life* and *love*. He gave us *light* in which we now stand. We no longer stand in the darkness, *but* we stand in His light, the heavenly glorious light full of grace and truth. Jesus said (John 8:12 NIV), "I am the light of this world. Whoever follows me will never walk in darkness but will have the light of life."

So, are we not Abraham's descendants through Jesus?

Are we not disciples of Jesus Christ?

Do we not receive blessings and promises from God through the *word*?

Yes, we are, and yes, we do!

Now let's take these blessings that have been so graciously given with love to us, and let's march forth through the darkness and rise up as Abraham and Jesus did. You might say, Abraham did not die and rise again. You are correct, but he did rise to the occasion when he was tested. He rose up to be obedient to His Lord, and he rose up in his faith! So yes, Abraham did rise up as he walked up the mountain with his son in strict adherence (obedience) to God, to give his one and only son as a burnt offering to the Lord.

So now let us rise up as Jesus did and share His love and His gospel, with wisdom and understanding. Let us move forward in the direction of His everlasting light, His everlasting life, His everlasting joy, and His everlasting love. Let's make our mark today as Jesus and his disciples did so many years ago. Let's make the message of Jesus come to life in the world today. How do we do this? First, we need to allow the Holy Spirit to come in and make contact with our spirit and join in our inheritance with the Lord. Second, we need to learn to rely on our spirit, *not* our flesh. When I speak of flesh, I am speaking of the physical body. We also need to cast down our thoughts, our imaginations, our negative words, in order to allow the Word of God to flow through our minds as they become renewed in Christ. We need to let the Word flow through us to let the body and blood of Jesus consume us. We need to let the Word come forth out of our mouth with a new light, love, and truth. This, my friend, is when we can experience the supernatural power of Jesus.

We are heirs with Jesus Christ, we are descendants of Abraham, and we are Sons of God. Yes, that is correct, Sons of God in training! (Galatians 4:6). Do you see the remarkable picture here? Do you see the possibilities that are at your right hand, through the Father in the Name of Jesus Christ? Do you see?

We are not to come with doubt in our hearts before our Lord, but we are to come *boldy* before Him (Hebrews 4:16 NIV). We are not to walk by flesh, but by spirit and by *love*. We are not to judge one another, but we are to *love* and *pray* for one another. Didn't Jesus give us the fruits and gifts that will help us in our walk with Him? Yes, he did. So why aren't we using them? (1 Corinthians 12).

We are not to walk in condemnation, but we are to walk in His *light* and shine His *light* with grace, mercy, and love upon others as he has done for us. We are to live in Jesus and walk with Him. We are to keep our eyes on Jesus and live in harmony with one another. Now, please don't misunderstand me; I never said this would be easy. We do have different seasons in our walk, different trials and tribulations that God may allow. Yes, I said *allow*, but I did not say He causes them. However, we may be attacked by Satan himself, but this doesn't mean that we give up or bow down to the enemy. What this does mean is we take the situation at hand and ask, "Lord, use this for good" (Genesis 50:15–21). Even though it was written in the Old Testament, it is still true today. God uses all for His good. God never fails us nor does he forsake us! He remains true to us because that is what *the word* tells us. He is love and He is truth! "Jesus Christ is the same yesterday and today and forever" (Hebrews 13:8 NIV). "I the Lord, do not change" (Malachi 3:6 NIV).

As we continue to grow in wisdom, understanding, and knowledge, and as we are shown deeper and deeper revelation, the stronger we become in our love walk. As our endurance strengthens, we will win the race that has been placed before us with grace, mercy, gratitude, and thanksgiving. Our reward is in heaven. Let's persevere in our goal to walk this love walk and defeat all darkness through the leading of the Holy Spirit, through wisdom, revelation, and understanding. Let's not fear darkness, for Jesus has already destroyed it. Let us walk in His light!

I am looking forward to the day when I stand face to face with Jesus and I am welcomed home. Are you? Won't it be exciting when we are rewarded for doing His will, His good deeds, and sharing Him with the world. I am reassured in my heart that when I stand face-to-face with Him that He will not tell me the He doesn't know me for we have a personal relationship. Do you? As stated in Matthew 7:22–23 (Amplified),

> Many will say to Me on that day [when I judge them], "Lord, Lord, have we not prophesied in Your name, and driven out demons in Your name, and done many miracles in Your Name?" And then I will declare to them publicly. "I never knew you; depart from me [you are banished from My presence], you who act wickedly [disregarding My commands]."

You see the nitty-gritty of this message is to be doers and lovers of the *word.* Now lovers of the word is showing grace, mercy, gratitude, thanksgiving, praise, and worship and being sons and daughters of Christ. We stand on the love meaning of God, not of the flesh. Our desires are not from God if they are of the flesh. How can we tell? We have peace within our hearts. Another way is to ask God. We always pray for the will of God. What is the will of God? It is in the *word.* Even Jesus didn't come in flesh to do His will, but the Father's will. That is what we are to be doing. We need to go to the Father in heaven daily, in Jesus's name, and ask him to show us how we can do better or have a better relationship with Him. And we can always do better, can't we?

So let us march forward with determination to walk in an intimate relationship with Jesus. And remember, our Father in heaven is our (daddy), and he will not fail us or forsake us. We should also try not to fail or forsake Him.

You see, it's easy to fall into temptation, sin and fall short on our prayer or love walk. But please remember, Jesus took all this from us. We don't need to hang onto our wrongdoings (our baggage), but we do need to move forward in order to confess and repent, forgive, and forget, and to love and stand in His light. Will the devil try to tempt us? Well, let us first examine, is it our flesh or the devil? How will we know? By checking our inner spirit, by communing with our Father, in Jesus's name, and by focusing on Jesus and not the devil. We have been given a Spirit of discerning, so let's use it. What is discerning? It is to distinguish or separate so as to investigate, to examine, to determine the excellence or defects of persons or things. It is a knowing from the Holy Spirit. As a matter of fact, magnify God the Father, God the Son, and God the Holy Spirit. Make them priority in your daily life, in your daily activities and routines, and in all you do. Make them number 1 always! For they are God, three in one. When you do this, it will knock down strongholds, it will knock down darkness, it will knock down religious spirits and all demons. God knocks down *all* darkness. You see when we don't keep our focus on Jesus, then we can accidentally open doors to all kinds of unwanted things. Rest assured, Jesus already dealt with darkness, and we no longer need to fear! We just use the sword of the spirit, which is *the word*, and all darkness and Satan must flee. And as a matter of fact, our flesh weakens. It really is that simple. Keep it simple. Remember darkness *cannot* defeat or penetrate His supernatural light. *And yes,* we can have that light too!

Do we have the right to judge others? Absolutely Not! Do we have the right to speak the *truth*? Absolutely! Yes, we do. What is the difference here then between judgment and speaking the truth? God is the one and only one who judges the world. Are there times we may need to bring light to another brother or sister? Yes, but we speak in truth and love. We pray and love one another. This is our only commandment is to love God with our whole heart, mind, soul, strength and to love one another (Mark 12:30 NIV). So then how do you think we could even begin to break the Ten Commandments? We can't if we're walking in love. As a matter of fact, darkness cannot be in us if we follow the love commandment. So you may say, what if we see a brother or sister committing a sin? Maybe they are walking in pride or self-righteousness or let's say not walking in the light and love? That is an easy answer. We love them, pray for them, and speak the truth to them. Now understand, this is for Christians. If they are not Christians, plant the seed, love, and pray for them and share Jesus. Please understand, it may not be by any words you speak, but it may certainly be by the light you shine! So, the next question. Do we hold Christians and non-Christians accountable? We don't, but God will and does.

Once again, we speak the truth, which is the Word. We act out the Word, and we are lovers of the Word. We keep our eyes on Jesus, and all else will fall into place. Should we fight with one another? No, but speak the truth by using the fruits of the spirit. We, my friends, should be doing as Jesus did and follow in His footsteps. We should follow the unction of the Holy Spirit. What is the unction? you might ask. It is the anointing of the Holy Spirit. Listen to your heart. Jesus didn't give us His Spirit to not use Him. He gave us His Spirit to be enlightened, to speak mysteries unto the Father in prayer, supplications, thanksgiving, praise, and worship (Philippians 4:5–8). He gave us the Holy Spirit to edify ourselves and become the best we can be. Don't let the Holy Spirit inside you be idle. The Holy Spirit keeps us in check; He warns us. He is our helper and advocate, comforter and counselor, teacher, standby, intercessor, and strengthener

(John 14:26). How can we go wrong with Him? We can't as long as we stay diligent and true to the Father, Son, and Holy Ghost.

Now keep in mind, Satan is the ruler of this world, so we may battle with principalities and powers, *but* remember this, Jesus has already conquered this for us! *always* keep this in your mind. Jesus is in your heart (if you've invited Him).

We are also protected under the Armor of God. Isn't that fascinating how God protects us? I am so grateful for His love. Let's look at this armor. We are covered by all parts of the armor except for the two-edged sword, which is His *word*, and that comes out of our mouth. He gave His *word*; He gave us Him to defeat any type of darkness. The girdle of truth protects us from Satan's lies. The breastplate of righteousness covers our hearts from all evil. When we put on the shoes of peace, we shine his light to everyone we encounter, and darkness cannot penetrate light. We pick up the shield of faith, which protects us from Satan's fiery darts of doubt, denial, and deceit. We put on the helmet of salvation, which covers our minds and thoughts, keeping us focused on the Word. As mentioned before, we use the sword of the spirit by speaking the Word, the Truth, and His love. God has us covered! Let's move forward with this armor in His light and His love and knock down darkness.

God has us in the palm of His hand, and he will never let us fail. Just remember who you are in Christ. Let's rise up as Abraham and Jesus did in the past and continue to walk in God's glory and His love. Let's magnify our awesome and amazing God. Let's move in this Jesus movement of this era. As we move forward, people will see His light within us, and they will want that same light that we have. His light will draw them in. They will want to receive His love and warmth that radiates from us. They will want Jesus!

Brothers and sisters in Christ, there is no better time than *now* to shine the light of life upon this world! Let's start today with a heavenly light that shines brighter and brighter with every step we take in Jesus. Let's walk forward with deeper understanding, wisdom, knowledge, and revelation of the Word. Let's follow the Holy Spirit who is our advocate, and trust in him! Let us move forward in God's love.

The Word never changes. Just like God has not changed. So if the Word has not changed and God has not changed, then this tells us that we still have the power, authority, and ability that they had back in the New Testament era, and we still have it today! Remember, Jesus went before us and took care of it all.

Isn't it amazing, when we are obedient and walk in the love of God, the blessings that we see and experience. It is easy, my friends, to get caught up in the world today. We have many desires of this world such as cars, technology, clothes, shoes, money, houses, property, etc. However, we also can have these blessings if we follow Jesus. He wants us to be rich in Him, and yes, we also can have the riches of the world *as long as* they don't have us. It is okay to have money, but it is not okay for money to have us. Do you see? Who is your God? Are you willing to move forward in your love walk today?

Rest assured, my friends, Jesus went before us, and that leads me to this next message from Jesus.

Don't Be Afraid

Have you ever asked yourself, "How can I go wrong, especially when Jesus gave me His life?" Have you ever really looked at yourself and realized what a wonderful new creation you have become, that He created you to be? Do you realize the special gift He has created for you? Jesus took it ALL, and He gave us *all.* What do I mean by this? Let's take a jaunt, if you will, down this narrow path of redemption to bring this picture deeper into His light.

One Sunday morning during church services, as we were singing the song "Be Not Afraid," the Lord brought a specific verse to my attention, which comes from Luke 6:20 and Isaiah 41:10, "Be Not Afraid." It has been over a year since He brought this verse to my attention, but now He has revealed the revelation pertaining to these scriptures. I now understand this revelation in such a deeper magnitude, and I would like to share it with you, if I may. Why? So you also have a better and deeper understanding of our Lord and Savior and how He works.

As it refers to in Deuteronomy 31:8 (NIV) and Isaiah 41:10 (NIV), "Be Not Afraid, I go before you always, come follow me, and I will give you rest." Wow! I never really gave this verse much thought, but as I was sitting there that one particular Sunday, the Lord magnified this verse for me, and I became fascinated. I became excited, but I didn't really know why. My heart leaped for joy! I didn't have an urge or unction, if you will. I just knew one day it would come to light. So I went home, wrote this verse down, and put it in the book of Luke. Of course, I came to it from time to time throughout the year during my Bible study. As I read it each time, I would say to the Lord, "Why did you have me write this down? Just curious." I would say with a smile. Well, as mentioned above, He finally explained it to me. He said to me, "What do you suppose that I am trying to tell you here? I am telling you to not be afraid. Why? Because I have given you ALL." He said, "Not only did I give it to you at pre-calvary, but also at calvary, and post-calvary. I created it for you from the beginning of time." He said, "Do you see?"

With much excitement, I said, "Yes, Lord, I do, and I have read and heard about your love and your sacrifice. I am willing to continue to learn and understand more and more day after day. Please share this understanding with me so that I may comprehend the depths of your love and mercy not only for myself but others as well."

You see, He has *always* given us His love. He gave us freedom. He gives each and every one of us second chances to change our thoughts, our ideas, and our life. As a matter of fact, He gives us chances upon chances beyond chances by demonstrating His grace and mercy upon each and every one of us. Mercy is His compassion and His love. He never leaves us nor forsakes us. Why? Because He went *before* us, leaving His footprints to guide us. Shall we follow? Yes, we shall. Do you see the importance of these statements?

Let's begin with John 18:15–27 and end with John 21:15–19. In these scriptures, it talks about Peter's denial of Jesus (pre-calvary). Now pay close attention. He prophesied that Peter would deny him three times. That is exactly what Peter did. His first denial of Jesus was when he was keeping warm by a fire when a servant girl asked him, "Aren't you one of the disciples?" And what did Peter say? "I am not." The second denial was still at the same location as Peter was warming himself, when he was asked again, "You aren't one of those disciples too, are you?" Peter answered, "I am not." The third denial came when one of the High Priest's servants, a relative of the man whose ear Peter had cut off, challenged him. "Didn't I see you with Him in the garden?" This was the third and last time Peter denied Him, and at that moment, the rooster crowed. You see, Jesus knew what was in Peter's heart, and He never gave up on him nor did He forsake him. Keep this in mind, for this is very important to remember.

Now let's talk about when Jesus reinstated Peter (post-calvary). Jesus asked Peter for the first time, "Simon, son of John, do you love me more than these?"

"Yes, Lord," he said. "You know that I love you."

Jesus said, "Feed My Lambs." Jesus asked Peter the second time, "Simon, son of John, do you love me?"

He said, "Yes, Lord, You know that I love you."

Jesus said, "Take care of my sheep." The third time, He said to him, "Simon, son of John, do you love me?"

Peter was hurt because Jesus asked him the third time, and he said, "Lord, you know all things. You know that I love you."

Jesus said, "Feed My Sheep."

Mind-blowing. Do you see what just happened here? Peter denied Jesus three times, and Jesus gave Peter the opportunity to reinstate himself with love. He gave him grace and mercy! These three confessions of love just counteracted the three denials of Jesus. What a major impact! What a statement of *love*, *grace*, and *mercy*. So why should we be afraid? Why should we fear? We should not. Remember Jesus knew us before creation. He is *always* before us. This is key.

Jesus loves us even when we deny him. You may say, "I have never denied Jesus." Let's get real with ourselves, shall we? You may not have denied Him with your mouth, but you most certainly denied Him with your fear. To be quite frank, we have denied our Father in heaven because we have denied His Son, whom we have denied with our actions and our fear. We, in our human flesh, certainly didn't understand this concept. *but* the special gift He so graciously has given us, the Holy Spirit, knew. I finally understood that denial isn't just denying His name, but it is denying what He has done for us and what He has given us. These statements bring light into our darkness.

Now, let's look at the difference between the world and sanctity (holiness). The time of the new birth, which is salvation, and the time of the Baptism of the Holy Spirit, which is the infilling of God's power. Oh, you see, yes, the new birth or new creation is when we receive salvation. The baptism of the Holy Spirit is when we receive the infilling of the Holy Spirit with evidence of speaking in tongues. So, prior to us becoming saved and being baptized with the infilling, we were given chances upon chances beyond chances as was bestowed upon Peter. Now mind you, the infilling can come upon you at the same time you receive salvation, by asking Jesus into your heart and entering into a personal relationship with Him. Sometimes, the infilling may come later. I believe this is up to that individual's thirst for the Lord. It states both instances in the Bible. However, this topic is for another time, because it's so amazing in its own right. There are many good resources out there on this topic. For now, we are focusing on love.

We should thank our Father for this deep revelation and deep understanding of His love and His mercy. He says, "Don't be afraid, I go before you always" (Deuteronomy 31:8). How *comforting*. He has given us His reassurance of His love, of His grace and mercy, and of His covenant with us.

We need not fear, for our Lord has taken down the obstacles that go before us in this world. How? He went before us! What obstacles? you might ask. The answer is the obstacles of the world, of the flesh, and of evil. He has shown us how to live. As a matter of fact, He has given us a part of Him that lives deep within our hearts, that leads us on the correct and narrow path. He gave us our inheritance. He is our *I am*, and He is in us and upon us. *Thank you, Jesus.* So, then I ask you again, why should you fear poverty, sickness and disease, pain, oppression, or whatever else the devil is trying to persuade you into? Why should you fear the darkness or the unknown? You see, Jesus has already provided for us *all* we need. He has given us the Holy Spirit, the true light, and He has given us the truth.

"Don't be afraid, I go before you always, come follow me, and I will give you rest." We have spoken of the reasons not to be afraid. What is the next step? "Come follow me." Let's look at Matthew 4:19. Jesus said, "Come follow me, and I will make you fishers of men." "Come follow me" is used throughout the gospels numerous times before the cross. Jesus asked us to follow Him after the cross when He provided us with the Holy Spirit. Remember, the Holy Spirit is our comforter and counselor, our helper and advocate, our intercessor and strengthener, and our standby (John 14:26). We are to follow Jesus as he has made the way for us. So again, why are we to follow Jesus? To be His light within the darkness, to help bring His children home, to preach and share the gospel (the Word), to exercise our authority, to see and do signs, wonders, and miracles, and to pray.

So therefore, it states, "Be Not Afraid." Why? Because He goes before us always. "Follow Him." Why? So He can give us rest. *Rest* in Greek means "to refresh." He is refreshing our souls. He is giving us His water so we can cross the finish line. So, as you can see, we need not fear, we need only to follow Him, and He will refresh us. How can you not be in *awe* right now?

Brothers and sisters, it is time *we get real* with ourselves and others as well. It is time to look at ourselves in the correct scheme of things and realize that we do not need to fear. Look at yourself in the mirror and own up to your fears and speak them out. Put them down once and for all. After all, Jesus went before us. To be frank again, we all have them no matter how long we have walked with Jesus, don't we? If you aren't truthful with yourself, then you certainly aren't being truthful with the Lord. *The good news is* that we no longer have to harbor our fears. Shout from the rooftops, "J*esus went before me. he did not leave me nor did he forsake me.*" Do you realize that He is our shield, our protector, and our healer? Thank you, Jesus.

Do not falter, rather focus on the *truth*. Focus on *jesus*, and keep your eyes fixed on what our Lord and Savior has done for us. He has given us His *life*. Now you may say, "Yes, yes, that all sounds good," or you may say, "I already know and understand this." But do you? In all reality, to what depth do you understand Him, to what depth do you seek Him? And to what depth do you *love* Him? Are you doers of the Word? Are you using the Word for growth? Remember this is all for your sake.

I can't express this enough! We need to keep learning every day, for we never outgrow the Word. We *must* stay in the Word and in Communion with Jesus daily. We must know who we truly are in Jesus Christ. Once again, you may say, "Yes, yes, I know this to be true." BUT do you in fact pray in the Spirit when times are tough?

Do you know that two in agreement means you and the Holy Spirit (the Lord) are in agreement? Do you know the importance of the Holy Spirit, really and truly? Start using your authority in Jesus and refuse—yes, *refuse* fear. Do not hesitate in any way, shape, or form. When a fear comes to your mind, shut it down! Why? For the Lord has already taken care of it as He went before us. **"Be not afraid, I go before you always, come follow me, and I will give you rest."**

Let's take our stand together to grow and grow and grow. Let's be the light in the darkness. Let's shine so bright that the Lord feels the warmth from inside and outside of us. Let's lead His children home. Let us partake in the knowledge, wisdom, understanding, and revelation of this verse, and realize the true nature of Jesus Christ our shield, our protector.

During any season of life, let's reflect on the pre-calvary, calvary, and post-calvary. Let's ask our Lord and Savior for deeper and deeper and deeper knowledge, understanding, wisdom, and revelation. He provides us rest. He has refreshed us *all.*

Listen to the Trees

Before I begin the conclusion of this journey, I want to express my love and gratitude to our Bible study crew. You are truly amazing women of God. I thank you for helping and teaching me in my walk with the Lord. I cannot even begin to express the joy I have when we gather together. You are all truly an inspiration. You use your God-given gifts, and that is an inspiration in itself. Thank you. Love you girls very much!

I am concluding this book on a psalm or song the Lord brought to me during a Bible study. I call this one "Listen to the Trees." It came out of nowhere with such a gentleness and passion. I just began speaking these words as they came to me during a Bible study meeting, and one of the women began to write them down. I am so very thankful for her writing this down, for at the time, I didn't understand the importance of this psalm. It is so amazing how God works His plans and how he has us all work together. I couldn't quite understand it then, but as I have grown in my faith, I am beginning to see the wonders of this psalm as it speaks to me. I hope and pray it brings revelation and healing to your hearts. It certainly has to mine, for it enlightens the story of our daughter with such a great love, *God's love.*

Listen to the trees. They have stories to tell of the Gospel.

Listen to the wind, feel the breeze, and taste the sap on your lips.

Feel the feathers of wisdom, taste the salt of the earth.

Hear the music play, touch with gentleness, see with your heart, and let the music play.

The tongue will speak of many things, have many thoughts, and say many prayers.

Take time out of your day, and listen to the trees. You will seek many treasures, you will hear wisdom.

Please light the world with your words, look to people with love, and bring them to me.

Let the music play. Sing joyfully.

Amen, I say this to you: pay attention, whisper sweet sounds, hush, and listen to the trees.

This I say to you in love. This I share, heed these words of wisdom.

Let the music play, let your heart fly like a dove, and let it land out in the sea. Let your wind (Spirit) take flight, for you are with me.

Praise Yahweh, sing to me.

Let your eyes and heart see the beauty. The words are there for you to see. Take heed and notice me, through the whispers of the trees.

Listen silently. No one needs to know you are listening. For I am with you. Shine your light on me. Sing to me, praise me, and worship me, and *listen to the trees.*

In ending the *Heart Beat of Love*, "Listen to the Trees" is an ode not only to Elly's journey but also to the lost. It is a psalm about our dear Lord's journey, and it is a message to us in our journeys. It is a message of beauty, of life, of love, and of our *creator*. It is a song of joy and laughter. It is the words of wisdom and solitude. It is Jesus who brings *life and love* to us all. Please know, whatever darkness you may be traveling through in this season of your life, Jesus is right there with you. You are never alone. You may not feel His presence, but that does not mean He is not there. As it states in Isaiah 30:15 (NIV), "In repentance and rest is your salvation. In quietness and trust is your strength."

I, my friends, believe wholly (completely) that God saved our daughter. He turned the bad into good, and He has brought us into a place in Him that is so pure. Yes, we miss Elly every day. But we know our daughter is home in the loving arms of Jesus, and she is safe and loved. One day, we will see Jesus face-to-face with such love and excitement! We will sense the power of His glorious *light* and His *love* on our face(s), and we will then know that we are home too. Oh the *joy*, oh the *refreshing*. And we will be united with Elly and with Him!

I give thanks to God the Father, God the Son, and God the Holy Spirit as I praise and worship Him, stand in love and agreement with Him, and stay in complete joy of *Him*.

This story, if you will, is the very message of God's love. It speaks of love, joy, miracles, and healing. It speaks of darkness, sadness, and fear. When we put these things into perspective, and when we are able to see the complete picture of our situation and lives, that is when our eyes are opened to His glorious light, His glorious love.

My prayer for you today and every day is this:

> Father in heaven, please extend your arms out to your people who are in need. For we are all in need of You. Hold them close to you, and never let them fall away in sadness, but carry them to their destination of joy. Let them find their peace in You and know that You are their God. I ask this in Your Glorious Son's Name, Jesus Christ. Amen.

I pray that all who read this book find many blessings and find peace in their inner beings. We, as people, all experience tests, trials, and tribulations. The key is how will you react or should I say praise in this situation. Sometimes it is so hard to see the light in the midst of darkness. Jesus said in John 8:12 (NIV), "I am the light of the world. Whoever follows me will never walk in darkness, but will have the light of life." Our response? "Yes, Jesus, You are the light, and I am following close behind you." Jesus also states in John 1:5 (NIV), "The Light shines in the darkness, and the darkness has not over come it." In your darkness, I challenge you to see the light today and every day. For as stated, Jesus who is the light is right beside you. He has never left you nor forsaken you.

Jesus also brings peace in His light. He states in John 14:27 (NIV), "Peace I leave with you; my peace I give to you. I do not give to you as the world gives. Do not let your hearts be troubled and do not be afraid." Let His peace come upon you and calm you in every season of your life, and let Him give you courage and strength for every endeavor. For He is our strength. He is our courage. He is our boldness. He is our path. He is our gateway to heaven. He is our Lord and Savior!

Take time today and be still and know that He is God.

My family and I have been so blessed, and we have found our peace. We take and look at each day as a new beginning a new adventure of life. Please don't misunderstand me, we are not perfect nor are we always where we should be or need to be. *But* Praise *Jesus*, we can always go to *Him*, in our time of need and in our time of joy, for He is our Lord and Savior. He is our *rest*. We find such peace in His presence, and I pray you all will find this love and peace in your lives.

Thank you for taking time to read the journey of our daughter's life and her road well traveled. As you can see, the *Heart Beat of Love* is a story of God's love.

May you always find comfort in God's love and peace and "Listen to the Trees."

All glory goes to God.

Resources and Definitions

Introduction page: This syndrome was first discovered by Dr. Pearson and his colleagues back in 1979 per the article on Pearson Marrow Pancreas Syndrome. The research and this article was written by Sara Seneca, Linda De Meirleir, Jean De Shepper, Nadine Balduck, Kristen Jochmans, Inge Liebaers, and Willy Lissens. This article was given to my husband and me by her hematologist when she was first diagnosed.

You may also wonder what is a mitochondrial disease (wikipedia.org). First, you need to understand what are mitochondria. To see the complete definition, you may find it on Wikipedia that explains this in full detail. However, once again, I am going to give you the understanding by a real-life experience and how this condition was explained to my husband and me by the medical field.

Mitochondria are small complex structures which exist in every cell of the body except for red blood cells. They are called the powerhouse of a cell because they produce most of the energy, which we all need to grow and live. So, the process which creates a disease is when the mitochondria are not working correctly together as they should.

Three months of age: A CBC is a complete blood workup that shows your WBC (white blood count), RBC (red blood count), HMG (hemoglobin), HCT (hematocrit), platelets, neutrophils (segs and bands), lymphocytes, and more. Her hemoglobin decreased to 7.1. A retic (reticulocytes) count was also completed. The retic count shows how many red blood cells are being produced by the bone marrow and released into the blood.

Four months of age: Electrolytes are made up of sodium, potassium, chloride, total carbon dioxide, and anion gap.

Eleven months of age: A G-J tube stands for gastrojejunostomy tube. She was now on IV fluids, which included the sodium bicarbonate, dextrose, and magnesium sulfate. This was the main solution for her IV bag. Peptamen Jr. with sodium bicarbonate was her food.

The other medications were Propulsid for her acid reflux, Carnivore for her mitochondrial cells, Viokase aids in digestion, Prilosec for reflux, Vitamin E and K for her blood, diet Sprite for flushing her feeding tube, Neupogen shot for white blood cells, and Cortef a steroid for her adrenal glands.

Twelve months of age: Titration was indicated for how many cc's per hour of IV solution and feeding solution, which is needed to receive in an hour's time. I also understood her needs. Between the IV fluids and feeds, they needed to total 60 cc per hour. For example, if her IV fluid was at 35 cc per hour, then her feeds needed to be titrated to 25 cc per hour to total the 60 cc per hour intake. Our goal was to eventually get her feeds up to 60 cc per hour and for her to maintain this amount.

One and only son: Dr. David Jeremiah in his book called *The Spiritual Warfare Answer Book* gives us "The Warrior Prayer" based on Ephesians 6:14–17.

The new year of love: White-Gray-Black Chart by acmg.seas.harvard.edu, GAMAP User Guide:

KJV/Amplified Parallel Bible by Zondervan. Copyright 2015 (copyright symbol goes here) by The Lockman Foundation. Amplified Bible. Copyright (copyright symbol goes here) 1954, 1958, 1962,1964, 1965, 1987, 2015 by The Lockman Foundation.

The Jeremiah Study Bible. Copyright (copyright symbol goes here) 2016 by David Jeremiah, Inc. by Worthy Publishing. (The Holy Bible, New International Version, NIV. Copyright [copyright symbol goes here] 1973, 1978, 1984, 2011 by Biblica, Inc. Used by permission of Zondervan).

Acknowledgments

Elly: I want to thank my daughter Elly for showing me what true unconditional love means, as God's love consumes us. I want to thank her for showing me the true meaning of what strength and courage is about. I want to thank her for the love and joy she brought to my life and our family's life. She was a true inspiration near and far. You see, sometimes you don't realize what you possess until you are faced with a trial. Rest assured, you can do all things through Christ who strengthens you (Philippians 4:13). I owe my children my life, for they have given me the most important gift, and that gift is their love. If we would just look through our children's eyes, which are their hearts, how better this world would be! You see, Elly led me to the love of God. God is love!

Steve: I want to thank my husband for being a very big part of me. I want to thank you for standing beside me in the good times and in the bad. I want to thank you for being full of love and compassion. Thank you for your support and shelter, for I find rest with you. Most of all, thank you for loving me. You have given and still give much of yourself to your children, grandchildren, and family. You are a wonderful husband, father, grandfather, father-in-law, brother, and brother-in-law. You are a very well-rounded person who is very giving and compassionate in all that you do. I thank you for standing beside me in this new journey that I am on. I love you.

Lindsey and Jesi: I want to thank our two very beautiful and spirit-filled daughters. I cannot thank you enough for knowing who you are in the Lord. I thank you for your understanding and patience as we walked through grief and joy. I know I wasn't always there for you through the days of Elly, and I know you were bearing the emotions as the rest of us were; however, you remained and still remain strong to this day. You remain full of compassion, mercy, and love, and these are qualities that are a gift from God. You shine your light, the light of Jesus, on everyone you come in contact with. Keep these qualities as you grow in your love walk. I love you.

Pediatrician and his staff and the medical field: I want to give you all a very special thank you from the bottom of my heart. I am reaching out to all of you who had a part to play in my daughter's care. You all gave yourselves without faltering. You gave our daughter Elly and her family complete respect, love, kindness, and generosity. You gave all these qualities with tenderness, compassion, and love. I thank you and please know you will never be forgotten, and you remain in my prayers and my heart. I believe Elly touched your heart as she has touched ours.

Family: I want to thank our family, relatives, and friends for all of your help, support, and prayers. You have given us so much love, and I want you to know that your thoughtfulness and kindness will always remain in our hearts. A special thank you goes out to my mom and dad, Elly's grandparents. Without you, we would not have been the family that we are today. We thank you for *always* being there for us with Elly and now. You are truly a Godsent, and we love you. Thank you for all of your love and support. We truly appreciate you, and we are blessed to have you in our lives. A special thank you for her uncle who gave her a very special gift, and that was his blood. We have no words to express our gratitude and love for you. Thank you! Thank you to my brothers, brothers-in-law, and sisters-in-law who stood beside us and loved us. I thank you for your help and understanding through that difficult time. Thank you to all of you who played a part in all areas of our lives during the Elly days and still play a part in our lives. We love you dearly, and you will remain in our hearts.

Prayer warriors: A special thank you for everyone who kept our daughter in their prayers. We do not know everyone who prayed for her, but we are so blessed to have people like you who take the time to show your compassion and love. Please know that your prayers were answered, although maybe not in the ways you expected. I believe we will find all our answers when we arrive at heaven's gates.

I thank you all for your love, support, and prayers. Please know you are greatly appreciated.

God the Father, God the Son, and God the Holy Spirit: I want to thank you for giving me the strength when I was weary and increasing my power when I was weak. For my hope was always in you, and you restored my strength. I soared on wings of eagles, I ran and did not grow weary, and I walked and did not grow faint (Isaiah 40:29–31). I thank you for answering my prayers. I thank you for being right beside me and my family. I know I prayed for the ultimate miracle for Elly's life to be saved, for her health to be restored. However, in fact, you *did* save her! You took her home to be with you. I know now that the devil is the one to blame. You see, God's will is healing and health. Jesus took our sins, our sickness, our pain, and so much more when he died on the cross. He gave up his spirit and said, "It Is Finished" (John 19:28–30). He gave us life, so why would He take it away? I don't believe for a moment that He causes sickness. I encourage each and every one who reads this to get into The Word (the Bible) and seek God the Father, God the Son, and God the Holy Spirit. Seek and be diligent, and you will find. It states, "Ask and it will be given to you; seek and you will find; knock and the door will be opened to you. For everyone who asks receives; the one who seeks finds; and to the one who knocks, the door will be opened" (Matthew 7:7–8 NIV). I saw miracles every day with Elly, and to this day, I am still seeing miracles. Thank you!

About the Author

The author's inspiration for a career as a registered nurse was birthed out of a painful yet beautiful walk with her daughter Elly, who battled a rare and deadly disease called Pearsons syndrome. She earned an associate degree in nursing science from the University of Pittsburgh. This path gave her a greater admiration for life, with a deeper walk in understanding, knowledge, compassion, and love. She carries these qualities not only for her family and friends but also for her patients and for the family members themselves who walk in the wave of their loved ones' sickness. She understands the depth of their sorrow and their joy because of her own rugged road that she traveled. She has worked in multiple fields of nursing, which include hospital emergency, psychiatric care, school nursing, and health/wellness. She also was a director of a program that bridged between physical and mental health arenas. She is the wife of an amazing and supportive husband, the mother of two beautiful faith-filled daughters, and she has been blessed with four beautiful and loving grandchildren. She and her husband live in a rural area in Pennsylvania.

CPSIA information can be obtained
at www.ICGtesting.com
Printed in the USA
BVHW080218260422
635015BV00001B/7

9 781638 448679